Praise for

The Ruthless Elimination of Hurry

"As someone all too familiar with 'hurry sickness,' I desperately needed this book."

—Scott Harrison, *New York Times* best-selling author of *Thirst*

"John Mark Comer is a hugely talented leader, speaker, and writer. You will find lots of wise advice here."

—Nicky Gumbel, vicar of Holy Trinity Brompton, London

"Necessary. Freeing."

—Annie F. Downs, best-selling author of *100 Days to Brave*

"Never has a generation needed a book as much as this. John Mark has beautifully written a remedy for our overworked and tired souls."

—Jeremy and Audrey Roloff, *New York Times* best-selling authors of *A Love Letter Life*

"Great guy; even better book!"

—Bob Goff, author of the *New York Times* bestsellers *Love Does* and *Everybody, Always*

"*The Ruthless Elimination of Hurry* is refreshing, revitalizing, and a shock to the system. Beautifully and compellingly written, it is a prophetic message for our time."

—Pete Greig, founder of the 24-7 Prayer movement and senior pastor of Emmaus Rd, Guildford, UK

"We've found no better conversation or antidote to our culture's problem of busyness and hurry than John Mark's words in this book. Beyond helpful and encouraging!"

—Alyssa and Jefferson Bethke, *New York Times* best-selling authors of *Love That Lasts*

"John Mark Comer has given a gift to the church. This book is prophetic, practical, and profoundly life giving. He confronts the idolatry of speed that is causing so much emotional and relational trauma, and he provides a way forward that creates hope, hunger, and a vision of a beautiful life."

—Jon Tyson, lead pastor of the Church of the City New York and author of *The Burden Is Light*

"John Mark Comer's transparency invites us to reconsider how we live our lives by getting straight to the point: if we don't eliminate our busyness, we just may eliminate our souls. *The Ruthless Elimination of Hurry* will inspire you to make the hard but practical choices that will utterly change your trajectory for the better."

—Gabe Lyons, president of Q Ideas

"Living as a spiritually and mentally healthy follower of Jesus in our technological, calendar-driven culture is, it turns out, quite difficult. In this book John Mark Comer shares a practical, personal, and challenging call to imagine new ways that our lives can imitate Jesus."

—Tim Mackie, cofounder of the Bible Project

John
Mark
Comer

The
Ruthless
Elimination
of
~~Hurry~~

Foreword
by
John
Ortberg

WATERBROOK

THE RUTHLESS ELIMINATION OF HURRY

All Scripture quotations, unless otherwise indicated, are taken from the Holy
Bible, New International Version®, NIV®. Copyright © 1973, 1978, 1984, 2011
by Biblica Inc.® Used by permission. All rights reserved worldwide. Scripture
quotations marked (ESV) are taken from the Holy Bible, English Standard
Version, ESV® Text Edition® (2016), copyright © 2001 by Crossway Bibles,
a publishing ministry of Good News Publishers. All rights reserved. Scripture
quotations marked (KJV) are taken from the King James Version. Scripture
quotations marked (MSG) are taken from The Message. Copyright © by Eugene
H. Peterson 1993, 1994, 1995, 1996, 2000, 2001, 2002. Used by permission of
NavPress. All rights reserved. Represented by Tyndale House Publishers Inc.

Italics in Scripture quotations reflect the author's added emphasis.

Hardcover ISBN 978-0-525-65309-7
eBook ISBN 978-0-525-65310-3

Copyright © 2019 by John Mark Comer

Design by Ryan Wesley Peterson
Author photo by Ryan Garber

Published in association with Yates & Yates, www.yates2.com

Published in the United States by WaterBrook, an imprint of Random House,
a division of Penguin Random House LLC.

WATERBROOK® and its deer colophon are registered trademarks of Penguin
Random House LLC.

Library of Congress Cataloging-in-Publication Data
Names: Comer, John Mark, 1980- author.
Title: The ruthless elimination of hurry : how to stay emotionally healthy and
    spiritually alive in the chaos of the modern world / John Mark Comer.
Description: First Edition. | Colorado Springs : WaterBrook, 2019.
Identifiers: LCCN 2019002924 | ISBN 9780525653097 (hardcover) | ISBN
    9780525653103 (electronic)
Subjects: LCSH: Simplicity—Religious aspects—Christianity. | Time—Religious
    aspects—Christianity. | Time management—Religious aspects—Christianity.
    | Mental health—Religious aspects—Christianity.
Classification: LCC BV4647.S48 C66 2019 | DDC 248.4/6—dc23
LC record available at https://lccn.loc.gov/2019002924

Printed in the United States of America
2019—First Edition

10 9 8 7 6 5 4 3 2 1

SPECIAL SALES
Most WaterBrook books are available at special quantity discounts when
purchased in bulk by corporations, organizations, and special-interest groups.
Custom imprinting or excerpting can also be done to fit special needs. For
information, please email specialmarketscms@penguinrandomhouse.com.

For Dallas Willard—thank you.

Come to me,
all you who are weary
and burdened,
and I will give you rest.
Take my yoke upon you
and learn from me,
for I am gentle
and humble in heart,
and you will find
rest for your souls.
For my yoke is easy
and my burden is light.

–Jesus in
Matthew 11v28–30

Foreword

The smartest and best man I have known jotted down some thoughts about hurry; I think they were posted in his kitchen when he died. "Hurry," he wrote, "involves excessive haste or a state of urgency. It is associated with words such as *hurl, hurdle, hurly-burly* (meaning "uproar"), and *hurricane.*" He defined it as a "state of frantic effort one falls into in response to inadequacy, fear, and guilt." The simple essence of hurry is *too much to do*! The good of being delivered from hurry is not simply pleasure but the ability to do calmly and effectively— with strength and joy—that which really matters. "We should take it as our aim," he wrote, "to live our lives entirely without hurry. We should form a clear intention to live without hurry. One day at a time. Trying today."

We should form a mental picture of our place in the world before God. This places us in a different context. Psalm 23 does not say "The Lord is my shepherd, therefore I gotta run faster." Shepherds rarely run. Good ones, anyway. He said to begin to eliminate things you "have" to do. He said it was important to not be afraid of "doing nothing." He said to plan on such times. He said it would be important to deal with the panic of not being busy. To allow yourself to be in the panic, feeling it roll over you, and not going for the fix.

John Mark Comer has written a prophetic word for our day. He is engaging and honest and learned and fun and humble. He guides us to a great crossroads. To choose to live an unhurried life in our day is somewhat like taking a vow of poverty in earlier centuries; it is scary. It is an act of faith. But there are deeper riches on the other side. To be in the presence of a person where hurry has (like Elvis) "left the building" is to be inspired about the possibility of another kind of Life.

I was struck by the gifts of wisdom studded throughout this book: "All my worst moments . . . are when I'm in a hurry." "Love, joy, and peace . . . are incompatible with hurry." "The average iPhone user touches his or her phone 2,617 times *a day*." (By way of contrast, the psalmist said, "I have set the LORD always before me" [Psalm 16v8, ESV]. What would my life be like if God touched my mind as frequently as I touch my phone?) Freedom perhaps never comes without great cost. And John Mark is someone who has made choices that involved a price, to pursue the life that is beyond price. He knows both the struggle and the choice, and so can speak to those of us who hunger and thirst.

Twenty centuries ago another wise man said, "[Make] the

best use of the time, because the days are evil" (Ephesians 5v16, ESV). I used to think that meant the days are full of sensuality and fleshly temptation. And of course, they are. But I think it mostly means that the life we were intended to live must be lived in time. And we are so used to spiritually mediocre days—days lived in irritation and fear and self-preoccupation and frenzy—that we throw our lives away in a hurry.

So, in these pages lies the Great Invitation. Take a deep breath. Put your cell phone away. Let your heart slow down. Let God take care of the world.

—John Ortberg

Prologue: Autobiography of an epidemic

It's a Sunday night, 10 p.m. Head up against the glass of an Uber, too tired to even sit up straight. I taught six times today—yes, *six*. The church I pastor just added *another* gathering. That's what you do, right? Make room for people? I made it until about talk number four; I don't remember anything after that. I'm well beyond tired—emotionally, mentally, even spiritually.

When we first went to six, I called up this megachurch pastor in California who'd been doing six for a while.

"How do you do it?" I asked.

"Easy," he said. "It's just like running a marathon once a week."

"Okay, thanks."

Click.

Wait . . . isn't a marathon really hard?

I take up long-distance running.

He has an affair and drops out of church.

That does not bode well for my future.

Home now, late dinner. Can't sleep; that dead-tired-but-wired feeling. Crack open a beer. On the couch, watching an obscure kung fu movie nobody's ever heard of. Chinese, with subtitles. Keanu Reeves is the bad guy.[1] Love Keanu. I sigh; lately, I'm ending most nights this way, on the couch, long after the family has gone to bed. Never been remotely into kung fu before; it makes me nervous. Is this the harbinger of mental illness on the horizon?

"It all started when he got obsessed with indie martial arts movies . . ."

But the thing is, I feel like a ghost. Half alive, half dead. More numb than anything else; flat, one dimensional. Emotionally I live with an undercurrent of a nonstop anxiety that rarely goes away, and a tinge of sadness, but mostly I just feel blaaah spiritually . . . empty. It's like my soul is hollow.

My life is so *fast*. And I like fast. I'm type A. Driven. A get-crap-done kind of guy. But we're well past that now. I work six days a week, early to late, and it's *still* not enough time to get it all done. Worse, I feel *hurried*. Like I'm tearing through each day, so busy with life that I'm missing out on the moment. And what is life but a series of moments?

Anybody? I can't be the only one . . .

Monday morning. Up early. In a hurry to get to the office. Always in a hurry. Another day of meetings. I freaking hate meetings. I'm introverted and creative, and like most millennials I get bored way too easily. Me in a lot of meetings is a terrible idea for all involved. But our church grew really fast, and that's part of the trouble. I hesitate to say this because, trust me, if anything, it's embarrassing: we grew by over a thousand people a year for seven years straight. I thought this was what I wanted. I mean, a fast-growing church is every pastor's dream. But some lessons are best learned the hard way: turns out, I don't actually *want* to be the CEO/executive director of a nonprofit/HR expert/strategy guru/leader of leaders of leaders, etc.

I got into this thing to teach the way of Jesus.

Is *this* the way of Jesus?

Speaking of Jesus, I have this terrifying thought lurking at the back of my mind. This nagging question of conscience that won't go away.

Who am I becoming?

I just hit thirty (level three!), so I have a little time under my belt. Enough to chart a trajectory to plot the character arc of my life a few decades down the road.

I stop.

Breathe.

Envision myself at forty. Fifty. Sixty.

It's not pretty.

I see a man who is "successful," but by all the wrong metrics: church size, book sales, speaking invites, social stats, etc., and the new American dream—your own Wikipedia page. In spite of all my talk about Jesus, I see a man who is emotionally unhealthy and spiritually shallow. I'm still in my marriage, but it's duty, not delight. My kids want nothing to do with the church; she was the mistress of choice for Dad, an illicit lover I ran to, to hide from the pain of my wound. I'm basically who I am today but older and worse: stressed out, on edge, quick to snap at the people I love most, unhappy, preaching a way of life that sounds better than it actually is.

Oh, and always in a *hurry*.

Why am I in such a rush to become somebody I don't even like?

It hits me like a freight train: in America you can be a success as a pastor and a failure as an apprentice of Jesus; you can gain a church and lose your soul.

I don't want this to be my life . . .

Fast-forward three months: flying home from London. Spent the week learning from my charismatic Anglican friends about life in the Spirit; it's like a whole other dimension to reality that I've been missing out on. But with each mile east, I'm flying back to a life I dread.

The night before we left, this guy Ken prayed for me in his posh English accent; he had a word for me about coming to a fork in the road. One road was paved and led to a city with lights. Another was a dirt road into a forest; it led into the dark, into the unknown. I'm to take the unpaved road.

I have absolutely no idea what it means. But it means *something,* I know. As he said it, I felt my soul tremor under God. But what is God saying to me?

Catching up on email; planes are good for that. I'm behind, as usual. Bad news again; a number of staff are upset with me. I'm starting to question the whole megachurch thing. Not so much the size of a church but the *way* of doing church.[2] Is this really it? A bunch of people coming to listen to a talk and then going back to their overbusy lives? But my questions come off angry and arrogant. I'm so emotionally unhealthy, I'm just leaking chemical waste over our poor staff.

What's that leadership axiom?

"As go the leaders, so goes the church."[3]

Dang, I sure hope our church doesn't end up like me.

Sitting in aisle seat 21C, musing over how to answer another tense email, a virgin thought comes to the surface of my mind. Maybe it's the thin atmosphere of thirty thousand feet, but I don't think so. This thought has been trying to break out for months, if not years, but I've not let it. It's too dangerous. Too much of a threat to the status quo. But the time has come for it to be uncaged, let loose in the wild.

Here it is: *What if I changed my life?*

Another three months and a thousand hard conversations later, dragging every pastor and mentor and friend and family member into the vortex of the most important decision I've ever made, I'm sitting in an elder meeting. Dinner is over. It's just me and our core leaders. This is the moment. From here on, my autobiography will fall into the "before" or "after" category.

I say it: "I resign."

Well, not resign per se. I'm not quitting. We're a multisite church. (As if one church isn't more than enough for a guy like me to lead.) Our largest church is in the suburbs; I've spent the last ten years of my life there, but my heart's always been in the city. All the way back to high school, I remember driving my '77 Volkswagen Bus up and down Twenty-Third Street and dreaming of church planting downtown.[4] Our church in the city is smaller. Much smaller. On *way* harder ground; urban Portland is a secular wunderland—all the cards are against you down here. But that's where I feel the gravity of the Spirit weighing on me to touch down.

So not resign, more like demote myself. I want to lead one church at a time. Novel concept, right? My dream is to slow down, simplify my life around abiding. Walk to work. I want to reset the metrics for success, I say. I want to focus more on who I am becoming in apprenticeship to Jesus. Can I do that?

They say yes.

(Most likely they are thinking, *Finally*.)

People will talk; they always do: He couldn't hack it (true). Wasn't smart enough (not true). Wasn't tough enough (okay, mostly true). Or here's one I will get for months: He's turning his back on God's call on his life. Wasting his gift in obscurity. Farewell.

Let them talk; I have new metrics now.

I end my ten-year run at the church. My family and I take a sabbatical. It's a sheer act of grace. I spend the first half comatose, but slowly I wake back up to my soul. I come back to a much smaller church. We move into the city; I walk to work. I start therapy. One word: *wow.* Turns out, I need a lot of it. I focus on emotional health. Work fewer hours. Date my wife. Play Star Wars Legos with my kids. (It's for them, really.) Practice Sabbath. Detox from Netflix. Start reading fiction for the first time since high school. Walk the dog before bed. You know, *live*.

Sounds great, right? Utopian even? Hardly. I feel more like a drug addict coming off meth. Who am I without the mega? A queue of people who want to meet with me? A late-night email flurry? A life of speed isn't easy to walk away from. But in time, I detox. Feel my soul open up. There are no fireworks in the sky. Change is slow, gradual, and intermittent; three steps forward, a step or two back. Some days I nail it; others, I slip back into hurry. But for the first time in years, I'm moving toward maturity, one inch at a time. Becoming more like Jesus. And more like my best self.

Even better: I feel God again.

I feel my own soul.

I'm on the unpaved road with no clue where it leads, but that's okay. I honestly value who I'm becoming over where I end up. And for the first time in years, I'm smiling at the horizon.

My Uber ride home to binge-watch Keanu Reeves was five years and as many lifetimes ago. So much has changed since then. This little book was born out of my short and mostly uneventful autobiography, my journey from a life of hurry to a life of, well, something else.

In a way, I'm the worst person to write about hurry. I'm the guy angling at the stoplight for the lane with two cars instead of three; the guy bragging about being the "first to the office, last to go home"; the fast-walking, fast-talking, chronic-multitasking speed addict (to clarify, not *that* kind of speed addict). Or at least I was. Not anymore. I found an off-ramp from that life. So maybe I'm the best person to write a book on hurry? You decide.

I don't know your story. The odds are, you aren't a former megachurch pastor who burned out and had a mid-life crisis at age thirty-three. It's more likely that you're a college student at USD or a twentysomething urbanite in Chicago or a full-time mom in Melbourne or a middle-aged insurance broker in Minnesota. Getting started in life or just trying to keep going.

The Korean-born German philosopher Byung-Chul Han ends his book *The Burnout Society* with a haunting observation of most people in the Western world: "They are too alive to die, and too dead to live."[5]

That was me to the proverbial T.

Is it you? Even a little?

We all have our own story of trying to stay sane in the day and age of iPhones and Wi-Fi and the twenty-four-hour news cycle and urbanization and ten-lane freeways with soul-crushing traffic and nonstop noise and a frenetic ninety-miles-per-hour life of go, go, *go* . . .

Think of this book like you and me meeting up for a cup of Portland coffee (my favorite is a good Kenyan from Heart on Twelfth) and me downloading everything I've learned over the last few years about how to navigate the treacherous waters of what French philosopher Gilles Lipovetsky calls the "hypermodern" world.[6]

But honestly: everything I have to offer you, I'm stealing from the life and teachings of Jesus of Nazareth, my rabbi, and so much more.

My favorite invitation of Jesus comes to us via Matthew's gospel:

> Come to me, all you who are weary and burdened, and I will give you rest. Take my yoke upon you and learn from me, for I am gentle and humble in heart, and you will find rest for your souls. For my yoke is easy and my burden is light.[7]

Do you feel "weary"?

What about "burdened"?

Anybody feel a bone-deep tiredness not just in your mind or body but in your *soul*?

If so, you're not alone.

Jesus invites all of us to take up the "easy" yoke. He has—on offer to all—an easy way to shoulder the weight of life with his triumvirate of love, joy, and peace. As Eugene Peterson translated Jesus' iconic line: "to live freely and lightly."[8]

What if the secret to a happy life—and it is a secret, an open one but a secret nonetheless; how else do so few people know it?—what if the secret isn't "out there" but much closer to home? What if all you had to do was slow down long enough for the merry-go-round blur of life to come into focus?

What if the secret to the life we crave is actually "easy"?

Now, let me clarify a few things before we begin:

First, I'm not you. While glaringly obvious, it needs to be said. I'm guessing this anti-hurry manifesto will grate on some of you; it did on me at first. It exposes the deep ache in all of us for a life that is different from the one we're currently living. The temptation will be to write me off as unrealistic or out of touch:

He has no idea what's it's like to be a single mom working two jobs just trying to pay off debt and make rent each week.

You're right; I don't.

He's woefully out of touch with life as an executive in the social Darwinism of the marketplace.

That might be true.

He doesn't get what it's like in my city/nation/generation.

I might not.

I simply ask you to hear me out.

Secondly, I'm not Jesus. Just one of his many apprentices who have been at it for a while. Again, obvious. My agenda for our time together is simple: to pass on some of the best things I've learned from sitting at the feet of the master. A man whose closest friends all said he was anointed with the oil of joy more than any of his companions.[9] My translation: he was the happiest person alive.

Most of us don't even *think* to look to Jesus for advice on how to be happy. For that we look to the Dalai Lama or our local mindfulness studio or Tal Ben-Shahar's positive psychology class at Harvard. They all have good things to say, and for that I'm grateful. But Jesus is in a class of his own; hold him up against any teacher, tradition, or philosophy—religious or secular, ancient or modern—from Socrates to the Buddha to Nietzsche to your yogi podcaster of choice. For me Jesus remains the most brilliant, most insightful, most thought-provoking teacher to ever walk the earth. And he walked *slowly* (more on that in a bit). So rather than buckle up, settle in.

On that note, finally, let me say it straight up: If you want Fast and Faster, this isn't the book for you. In fact, you don't really have time to read a book; maybe skim the first chapter? Then you'd better get back at it.

If you want a quick fix or a three-step formula in an easy acronym, this book isn't for you either. There's no silver bullet for life. No life hack for the soul. Life is extraordinarily complex. Change is even more so. Anybody who says differently is selling you something.

But . . .

If you're weary . . .

If you're tired of life as you know it . . .

If you have a sneaking suspicion that there might be a better way to be human . . .

That you might be missing the whole point . . .

That the metrics for success our culture handed you might be skewed . . .

That said "success" might turn out to look a lot like failure . . .

Above all, if your time has come and you're ready to go on a counterintuitive and *very* countercultural journey to explore your soul in the reality of the kingdom . . .

Then enjoy the read. This book isn't long or hard to understand. But we have secrets to tell . . .

Part one:

The problem

Hurry: the great enemy of spiritual life

Last week I had lunch with my mentor John. Okay, confession: he's not actually my mentor; he's way out of my league, but we regularly have lunch and I ask a barrage of questions about life, notepad open. John is the kind of person you meet and immediately think, *I want to be like that when I grow up.* He's blisteringly smart but more—wise. Yet he never comes off remotely pretentious or stuck up. Instead, he's joyful, easygoing, comfortable in his own skin, a raging success (but not in that annoying celebrity way), kind, curious, present to you and the moment . . . Basically, he's a lot like how I imagine Jesus.[1]

John (last name Ortberg) happens to be a pastor and writer in California who was mentored by another hero of mine, Dallas Willard. If you don't know that name, you're welcome.[2] Willard was a philosopher at the University of Southern

California but is best known outside academia as a teacher of the way of Jesus. More than any teacher outside the library of Scripture, his writings have shaped the way I follow—or as he would say, apprentice under—Jesus.[3] All that to say, John was a mentee of Willard for over twenty years, until Willard's death in 2013.

I never got the chance to meet Willard, so the first time John and I sat down in Menlo Park, I immediately started pumping him for stories. We hit gold.

Here's one I just can't stop thinking about:

John calls up Dallas to ask for advice. It's the late '90s, and at the time John was working at Willow Creek Community Church in Chicago, one of the most influential churches in the world. John himself is a well-known teacher and best-selling author—the kind of guy you figure pretty much has apprenticeship to Jesus *down.* But behind the scenes he felt like he was getting sucked into the vortex of megachurch insanity.

I could relate.

So he calls up Willard and asks, "What do I need to do to become the me I want to be?"[4]

There's a long silence on the other end of the line . . .

According to John, "With Willard there's *always* a long silence on the other end of the line."

Then: "You must ruthlessly eliminate hurry from your life."

Can we just hit stop for a minute and agree, that's *brilliant*?

Thanks . . .

John then scribbles that line down in his journal—sadly this was before Twitter; otherwise that would have broken the internet. Then he asks, "Okay, what else?"

Another long silence . . .

Willard: "There is nothing else. Hurry is the great enemy of spiritual life in our day. You must ruthlessly eliminate hurry from your life."

End of story.[5]

When I first heard that, I felt a deep resonance with reality. Hurry is the root problem underneath so many of the symptoms of toxicity in our world.

And yet Willard's reply is not what I would expect. I live in one of the most secular, progressive cities in America, but if you were to ask me, What is the great challenge to your spiritual life in Portland? I'm not sure what I'd say.

Most likely I'd say it's modernity or postmodernity or liberal theology or the popularization of the prosperity gospel or the redefinition of sexuality and marriage or the erasure of gender or internet porn or the millions of questions people have about violence in the Old Testament or the fall of celebrity pastors or Donald Trump. I don't know.

How would you answer that question?

I bet very few of us would default to "hurry" as our answer.

But read the Bible: Satan doesn't show up as a demon with a pitchfork and gravelly smoker voice or as Will Ferrell with an electric guitar and fire on *Saturday Night Live.* He's far more intelligent than we give him credit for. Today, you're far more likely to run into the enemy in the form of an alert on your phone while you're reading your Bible or a multiday Netflix binge or a full-on dopamine addiction to Instagram or a Saturday morning at the office or *another* soccer game on a Sunday or commitment after commitment after commitment in a life of speed.

Corrie ten Boom once said that if the devil can't make you sin, he'll make you busy. There's truth in that. Both sin and busyness have the exact same effect—they cut off your connection to God, to other people, and even to your own soul.

The famous psychologist Carl Jung had this little saying:

Hurry is not *of* the devil; hurry *is* the devil.

Jung, by the way, was the psychologist who developed the framework of the introvert and extrovert personality types and whose work later became the basis for the Myers-Briggs

Type Indicator test. (INTJ, anybody?) Suffice to say: he knew what he was talking about.

Recently I was running the vision of our church by my therapist, who is this Jesus-loving, ubersmart PhD. Our dream was to re-architect our communities around apprenticeship to Jesus. (That feels so odd to write because what else would we be doing as a church?) He loved it but kept saying the same thing: "The number one problem you will face is *time.* People are just too busy to live emotionally healthy and spiritually rich and vibrant lives."

What do people normally answer when you ask the customary, "How are you?"

"Oh, good—just *busy.*"

Pay attention and you'll find this answer everywhere—across ethnicity, gender, stage of life, even class. College students are busy. Young parents are busy. Empty nesters living on a golf course are busy. CEOs are busy; so are baristas and part-time nannies. Americans are busy, Kiwis are busy, Germans are busy—we're *all* busy.

Granted, there is a healthy kind of busyness where your life is full with things that matter, not wasted on empty leisure or trivial pursuits. By that definition Jesus himself was busy. The problem isn't when you have a lot to do; it's when you have *too much* to do and the only way to keep the quota up is to hurry.

That kind of busy is what has us all reeling.

Michael Zigarelli from the Charleston Southern University School of Business conducted the Obstacles to Growth Survey of over twenty thousand Christians across the globe and identified busyness as a major distraction from spiritual life. Listen carefully to his hypothesis:

> It may be the case that (1) Christians are assimilating to a culture of busyness, hurry and overload, which leads to (2) God becoming more marginalized in Christians' lives, which leads to (3) a deteriorating relationship with God, which leads to (4) Christians becoming even more vulnerable to adopting secular assumptions about how to live, which leads to (5) more conformity to a culture of busyness, hurry and overload. And then the cycle begins again.[6]

And pastors, by the way, are the worst. He rated busyness in my profession right up there with lawyers and doctors.

I mean, not me. *Other* pastors . . .

As the Finnish proverb so eloquently quips, "God did not create hurry."

This new speed of life isn't Christian; it's anti-Christ. Think about it: What has the highest value in Christ's kingdom economy? Easy: love. Jesus made that crystal clear. He said the greatest command in all of the Torah was to "love the Lord your God with all your heart and with all your soul . . . and with all your strength," followed only by, "love your neighbor as yourself."[7] But love is painfully time consuming. All parents know this, as do all lovers and most long-term friends.

Hurry and love are incompatible. All my worst moments as a father, a husband, and a pastor, even as a human being, are when I'm in a hurry—late for an appointment, behind on my unrealistic to-do list, trying to cram too much into my day. I ooze anger, tension, a critical nagging—the antitheses of love. If you don't believe me, next time you're trying to get your type B wife and three young, easily distracted children out of the house and you're running late (a subject on which I have a wealth of experience), just pay attention to how you relate to them. Does it look and feel like love? Or is it far more in the vein of agitation, anger, a biting comment, a rough glare? Hurry and love are oil and water: they simply do not mix.

Hence, in the apostle Paul's definition of *love,* the first descriptor is "patient."[8]

There's a reason people talk about "walking" with God, not "running" with God. It's because God is love.

In his book *Three Mile an Hour God,* the late Japanese theologian Kosuke Koyama put this language around it:

> God walks "slowly" because he is love. If he is not love he would have gone much faster. Love has its speed. It is an inner speed. It is a spiritual speed. It is a different kind of speed from the technological speed to which we are accustomed. It is "slow" yet it is lord over all other speeds since it is the speed of love.[9]

In our culture *slow* is a pejorative. When somebody has a low IQ, we dub him or her slow. When the service at a restaurant is lousy, we call it slow. When a movie is boring, again, we complain that it's slow. Case in point, *Merriam-Webster:* "mentally dull: stupid: naturally inert or sluggish: lacking in readiness, promptness, or willingness."[10]

The message is clear: slow is bad; fast is good.

But in the upside-down kingdom, our value system is turned on its head: hurry is of the devil; slow is of Jesus, because Jesus is what love looks like in flesh and blood.

The same is true for joy and peace—two of the other core realities of the kingdom. Love, joy, and peace are the triumvirate at the heart of Jesus's kingdom vision. All three are more than just emotions; they are overall conditions of the heart. They aren't just pleasant feelings; they are the kinds of people we become through our apprenticeship to Jesus, who embodies all three ad infinitum.

And all three are incompatible with hurry.

Think of joy. All the spiritual masters from inside and outside the Jesus tradition agree on this one (as do secular psychologists, mindfulness experts, etc.): if there's a secret to happiness, it's simple—presence to the moment. The more present we are to the now, the more joy we tap into.

And peace? Need I even make a case? Think of when you're in a hurry for your next event, running behind: Do you feel the deep shalom of God in your soul? A grounded, present sense of calm and well-being?

To restate: love, joy, and peace are at the heart of all Jesus is trying to grow in the soil of your life. And all three are incompatible with hurry.

Again, if you don't believe me, next time you're dragging the family (or if you're single, the roommate) out the door, pay attention to your heart. Is it love and joy and peace you feel? Of course not.

At lunch my non-mentor mentor John wisely observed: "I cannot live in the kingdom of God with a hurried soul."

Nobody can.

Not only does hurry keep us from the love, joy, and peace of the kingdom of God—the very core of what all human beings crave—but it also keeps us from *God himself* simply by stealing our attention. And with hurry, we always lose more than we gain.

Here for the win, Walter Adams, the spiritual director to C. S. Lewis:

> To walk with Jesus is to walk with a slow, unhurried pace. Hurry is the death of prayer and only impedes and spoils our work. It never advances it.[11]

Meaning, very little can be done with hurry that can't be done better without it. Especially our lives with God. And even our work *for* God.

Here from Ronald Rolheiser, my undisputed favorite Catholic writer of all time, with hurricane force:

> Today, a number of historical circumstances are blindly flowing together and accidentally conspiring to produce a climate within which it is difficult not just to think about God or to pray, but simply to have any interior depth whatsoever. . . .
>
> We, for every kind of reason, good and bad, are distracting ourselves into spiritual oblivion.
>
> It is not that we have anything against God, depth, and spirit, we would like these, it is just that we are habitually too preoccupied to have any of these show up on our radar screens. We are more busy than bad, more distracted than nonspiritual, and more interested in the movie theater, the sports stadium, and the shopping mall and the fantasy life they produce in us than we are in church. Pathological busyness, distraction, and restlessness are major blocks today within our spiritual lives.[12]

I love Rolheiser's turn of phrase: "pathological busyness."

Again, a certain level of busyness is fine or at least unavoidable.

There's even a time and place for hurry—in a 911-caliber emergency, when your wife's water breaks or your toddler runs into the street.

But let's be honest: those moments are few and far between. The pathological busyness that most of us live with as our default setting, the chronic hurry we assume is normal, is far more, well, pathological, as in the technical sort: a pathogen let loose into a mass population, resulting in disease or death.

We hear the refrain "I'm great, just busy" so often we assume pathological busyness is okay. After all, everybody else is busy too. But what if busyness isn't healthy? What if it's an airborne contagion, wreaking havoc on our collective soul?

Lately I've taken to reading poetry, which is new for me. But I love how it forces me to slow down. You simply can't speed-read a good poem. Last night I picked up the Christian savant and literary master T. S. Eliot. A little of it I even understood, like his line about "this twittering world" where people are "distracted from distraction by distraction."[13] Meaning, a world with just enough distraction to avoid the wound that could lead us to healing and life.

Again: We are "distracting ourselves into spiritual oblivion."

As Ortberg has said,

> For many of us the great danger is not that we will renounce our faith. It is that we will become so distracted and rushed and preoccupied that we will settle for a mediocre version of it. We will just skim our lives instead of actually living them.[14]

Do you see what's at stake here? It's not just our emotional health that's under threat. As if that's not enough. We move so fast through life that we're stressed out, on edge, quick to snap at our spouses or kids. Sure, that's true. But it's even more terrifying: our spiritual lives hang in the balance.

Could it be that Willard was right? That an overbusy, digitally distracted life of speed is the greatest threat to spiritual life that we face in the modern world?

I can't help but wonder if Jesus would say to our entire generation what he said to Martha: "You are worried and upset about many things, but few things are needed—or indeed only one."[15]

The need of the hour is for a slowdown spirituality.[16]

A brief history of speed

We all know our world has sped up to a frenetic pace. We feel it in our bones, not to mention on the freeway. But it hasn't always been this way.

Let me nerd out on you for a few minutes just to show you how we got here. We'll talk about the Roman sundial, Saint Benedict, Thomas Edison, your toaster, 1960s sci-fi, 7-Eleven, and, naturally, Steve Jobs.

First, the sundial, aka the original Casio.

As far back as approximately 200 BC,[1] people were complaining about what this "new" technology was doing to society. The Roman playwright Plautus turned anger into poetry:

The gods confound the man who first found out
How to distinguish hours! Confound him, too,
Who in this place set up a sun-dial
To cut and hack my days so wretchedly
Into small portions![2]

Next time you're running late, just quote a little Plautus.

The gods confound the man!

Fast-forward to the monks, our well-meaning spiritual ances-
tors who played a key role in the acceleration of Western
society. In the sixth century Saint Benedict organized the
monastery around seven times of prayer each day, a super-
lative idea. By the twelfth century the monks had invented
the mechanical clock to rally the monastery to prayer.

But most historians point to 1370 as the turning point in the
West's relationship to time. That year the first public clock
tower was erected in Cologne, Germany.[3] Before that, time
was natural. It was linked to the rotation of the earth on its
axis and the four seasons. You went to bed with the moon
and got up with the sun. Days were long and busy in summer,
short and slow in winter. There was a rhythm to the day and
even the year. Life was "dominated by agrarian rhythms, free
of haste, careless of exactitude, unconcerned by productivity,"[4] in the words of the French medievalist Jacques Le
Goff. (And yes, I just quoted a French medievalist.)

But the clock changed all that: it created artificial time—the
slog of the nine-to-five *all year long.* We stopped listening to
our bodies and started rising when our alarms droned their

oppressive siren—not when our bodies were done resting. We became more efficient, yes, but also more machine, less human being.

Listen to one historian's summary of this key moment:

> Here was man's declaration of independence from the sun, new proof of his mastery over himself and his surroundings. Only later would it be revealed that he had accomplished this mastery by putting himself under the dominion of a machine with imperious demands all its own.[5]

When the sun set our rhythms of work and rest, it did so under the control of God; but the clock is under the control of the employer, a far more demanding master.

Then in 1879 you had Edison and the light bulb, which made it possible to stay up past sunset. Okay, brace yourself for this next stat: before Edison the average person slept eleven hours a night.[6]

Yes: *eleven.*

I used to read biographies of great men and women from history who got up to pray at four o'clock in the morning— Saint Teresa of Ávila, John Wesley, Charles Spurgeon. I would think, *Wow, they are* way *more serious about Jesus than I am.* True, but then I realized that they went to bed at seven o'clock! After nine hours of sleep, what else was there to do?

Now, at least in America, we're down to about seven as the

median number of hours of sleep per night. That's two and a half hours less sleep than just a century ago.

Is it any wonder we're exhausted all the time?

About a century ago technology started to change our relationship to time yet again, this time with so-called labor-saving devices.

For example, in winter you used to have to go out into the forest, risk being eaten alive by a wild animal, chop a tree down with an ax using your bare hands, drag the tree back to your cabin, chop it into pieces, and then make a fire, again with your bare hands. Now all you have to do is walk over to the thermostat on the wall (or, if you have a smart home, on your phone) and push the up arrow. *Voilà.* Warm air magically appears.

Examples are legion: We used to walk everywhere; now we have cars to get from place to place in a hurry. We used to make all our food from scratch; now we have takeout. We used to write letters by hand; now we have email and of course, our new best friend, AI.

Yet in spite of our smartphones and programmable coffee-pots and dishwashers and laundry machines and toasters, most of us feel like we have *less* time, not more.

What gives?

Labor-saving devices really do save time. So where did all that time go?

Answer: we spent it on other things.

In the 1960s futurists all over the world—from sci-fi writers to political theorists—thought that by now we'd all be working *way* fewer hours. One famous Senate subcommittee in 1967 was told that by 1985, the average American would work only twenty-two hours a week for twenty-seven weeks a year. Everybody thought the main problem in the future would be too much leisure.[7]

Wha . . . ?

Are you laughing right now? Yeah, it's funny, kind of.

Unless you're French (to all three of my French readers, we mock you, but it's only because we're jealous),[8] the exact opposite has happened: leisure time has gone *down.* The average American works nearly four more weeks per year than they did in 1979.[9]

Harvard Business Review recently conducted a study on the change in social status in America. It used to be that leisure was a sign of wealth. People with more money spent their time playing tennis or sailing in the bay or sipping white wine during lunch at the golf club. But that's changed. Now *busyness* is a sign of wealth. You see this cultural shift in advertising. Commercials and magazine ads for luxury items like a Maserati or a Rolex used to show the rich sitting by a pool in the south of France. Now they are more likely to show the wealthy in New York or downtown LA leading a meeting from a high-rise office, going out for late-night drinks at a trendy club, or traveling the world.[10]

A century ago the less you worked, the *more* status you had. Now it's flipped: the more you sit around and relax, the *less* status you have.

Not surprisingly, over this same time period we've seen the death of the Sabbath in American life. Until the 1960s (and in some places, as recently as the '90s), blue laws forced businesses to close on the Sabbath, a government-mandated speed limit on the pace of American life. My dad is pushing seventy, and he tells stories about growing up in the Bay Area in the '50s and how the entire city would shut down at six on weekdays and all day on Sundays. *Nothing* was open but the church. Nobody went out to brunch or to a sports game, much less shopping. Can you imagine that happening in Silicon Valley today? I can't. My dad still talks about what a big deal it was when 7-Eleven came to town—the first chain store to stay open seven days a week. And until 11 p.m.! In one generation, Sunday evolved from a day of rest and worship to a day to buy more crap we don't need, run errands, eat out, or just get a jump-start on our work for the week ahead.

Our culture never even slowed down long enough to ask, What will this new pace of life do to our souls?

Andrew Sullivan, in an essay for *New York Times Magazine* entitled "I Used to Be a Human Being," had this provocative analysis:

> That Judeo-Christian tradition recognized a critical distinction—and tension—between noise and silence,

between getting through the day and getting a grip on one's whole life. The Sabbath—the Jewish institution co-opted by Christianity—was . . . a moment of calm to reflect on our lives under the light of eternity. It helped define much of Western public life once a week for centuries—only to dissipate, with scarcely a passing regret, into the commercial cacophony of the past couple of decades. It reflected a now-battered belief that a sustained spiritual life is simply unfeasible for most mortals without these refuges from noise and work to buffer us and remind us who we really are.[11]

We lost more than a day of rest; we lost a day for our souls to open up to God.

All of this reached a climax in 2007. When the history books are written, they will point to '07 as an inflection point on par with 1440.

And 1440, of course, was the year Johannes Gutenberg invented the printing press, which set the stage for the Protestant Reformation and the Enlightenment, which to-gether transformed Europe and the world.

And 2007? Drumroll . . . The year Steve Jobs released the iPhone into the wild.

Note: it was also a few months after Facebook opened up to anybody with an email address, the year a microblogging app called Twitter became its own platform, year one of the cloud, along with the App Store, the year Intel switched from silicon to metal chips to keep Moore's law on a roll, and a list of other technological breakthroughs—all right around 2007, the official start date of the digital age.[12]

The world has radically changed in a few short years. In very recent memory none of us had a smartphone or Wi-Fi access. Now we can't imagine living without something that didn't even exist when my first child was born.

The internet alone has changed the world, and not just for the better. Depending on who you talk to, it's *decreasing* our IQs or at least our capacity to pay attention.

It's a bit dated now, but Nicholas Carr's Pulitzer Prize–nominated book *The Shallows: What the Internet Is Doing to Our Brains* is still the seminal work on this evolution (or devolution?). He wrote:

> What the Net seems to be doing is chipping away my capacity for concentration and contemplation. Whether I'm online or not, my mind now expects to take in information the way the Net distributes it: in a swiftly moving stream of particles. Once I was a scuba diver in the sea of words. Now I zip along the surface like a guy on a Jet Ski.[13]

And the smartphone put the internet in our front right pockets.

A recent study found that the average iPhone user touches his or her phone 2,617 times *a day.* Each user is on his or her phone for two and a half hours over seventy-six sessions.[14]

And that's for *all* smartphone users. Another study on millennials put the number at twice that.[15] In every study I read, most people surveyed had no clue how much time they actually lost to their phones.[16]

A similar study found that just being in the same *room* as our phones (even if they are turned off) "will reduce someone's working memory and problem-solving skills." Translation: they make us dumber. As one summary of the report put it, "If you grow dependent on your smartphone, it becomes a magical device that silently shouts your name at your brain at all times."[17]

And that's just our phone use—posting on social media, checking our email, looking up the weather, etc. Those stats don't even touch on internet use, much less the fire-breathing dragon of Netflix. So much time is lost in the black hole of the "device."

There's a Silicon Valley insider named Tristan Harris doing some really interesting work right now. Labeled by the *Atlantic* as "the closest thing Silicon Valley has to a conscience," he points out that slot machines make more money than the film industry and baseball *combined,* even though they take only a few quarters at a time. Because the slot machine is addictive. And those small amounts of money feel inconsequential in the moment. It's just a few quarters, right? Or five bucks, or twenty. But over time they add up. In the same way, the phone is addictive. And small moments—a text here, a scroll through Instagram there, a quick email scan, dinking around online—it all adds up to an extraordinary amount of time.[18]

Harris was a design ethicist and product philosopher (yes, that's a thing) for Google but grew disenfranchised with the tech industry. He left and started a nonprofit with the sole goal of advocating for a Hippocratic oath for software designers, because right now everything is being *intentionally designed for distraction and addiction.* Because that's where the money is.

Another example: Sean Parker, the first president of Facebook (played by Justin Timberlake in the movie), now calls himself a "conscientious objector" to social media. In an interview with Axios, he begrudgingly admitted:

> God only knows what it's doing to our children's brains. The thought process that went into building these applications, Facebook being the first of them, . . . was all about: *"How do we consume as much of your time and conscious attention as possible?"* And that means that we need to sort of give you a little dopamine hit every once in a while, because someone liked or commented on a photo or a post or whatever. And that's going to get you to contribute more content, and that's going to get you . . . more likes and comments. It's a social-validation feedback loop . . . exactly the kind of thing that a hacker like myself would come up with, *because you're exploiting a vulnerability in human psychology.*[19]

I added the italics, but in moments like these we see behind the curtain of what my friend Mark Sayers calls "digital capitalism." Economists call it the "attention economy." Harris calls it an "arms race for people's attention." A company can get your money if, *and only if,* they can get your attention.

Cue a terrifying trend: our attention span is dropping with each passing year. In 2000, before the digital revolution, it was twelve seconds, so it's not exactly like we had a lot of wiggle room. But since then it's dropped to eight seconds.

To put things in perspective, a goldfish has an attention span of nine seconds.[20]

Yes. That's right. We're losing, to *goldfish.*

But the odds are not in our favor. There are literally thousands of apps and devices *intentionally engineered* to steal your attention. And with it your money.

Reminder: Your phone doesn't actually work for you. You pay for it, yes. But it works for a multibillion-dollar corporation in California, not for you. You're not the customer; you're the product. It's your attention that's for sale, along with your peace of mind.[21]

And Harris isn't the only refusenik in tech. Nor am I the only pastor to sound the alarm.[22] Stories are leaking out of Silicon Valley of tech executives paying through the roof for a device-free private school for little Jonny, the epitome of Biggie Smalls's maxim: "Never get high on your own supply."

James Williams called the tech industry "the largest, most standardised and most centralised form of attentional control in human history."[23]

Microsoft researcher Linda Stone said "continuous partial attention" is our new normal.[24]

The sci-fi writer Cory Doctorow said every time we pick up our phones or go online, we're dropped into an "ecosystem of interruption technologies."[25]

Before *any* of this started, way back in 1936, another literary prophet, Aldous Huxley, wrote of "man's almost infinite appetite for distractions."[26] In his prescient novel *Brave New World,* he envisioned a future dystopia not of dictatorship but of distraction, where sex, entertainment, and busyness tear apart the fabric of society.

It's almost like he was onto something . . .

The problem is, even if we realize and admit that we have a digital addiction—it's an *addiction.* Our willpower doesn't stand a chance against the Like button.

And that's if we even admit we have a problem; most of us won't.

Psychologists make the point that the vast majority of Americans' relationship to their phones falls at least under the category of "compulsion"—we *have* to check that last text, click on Instagram, open that email, etc. But most of us are past that to full-on addiction.

As Tony Schwartz said in his opinion piece for the *New York Times:*

> Addiction is the relentless pull to a substance or an activity that becomes so compulsive it ultimately inter-

feres with everyday life. By that definition, nearly everyone I know is addicted in some measure to the Internet.[27]

Everyone.

If you think you're the exception to the rule, great—*prove it.* How? Turn off your phone for twenty-four hours straight. Just one day. Call it a digital Sabbath. See if you can make it that long without giving in to the itch to pick your phone back up or without writhing on the floor in a cold sweat with your teeth chattering from neurobiological withdrawal.

My point here isn't to advocate for a Luddite return to some mythical pre-digital utopia. The idea of farming for a few decades and then dying of gout sounds, well, horrible. And can you imagine life without Maps? Terrifying. No Apple Music? I shudder. All I'm saying is that we talk constantly about the pros of the modern digital age—and there are many—but we rarely say anything about the cons. Is it even a net positive?

Neil Postman, another prescient thinker, well ahead of his time, gave this prophetic warning for our day:

> Technology must never be accepted as part of the natural order of things. . . . Every technology—from an IQ test to an automobile to a television set to a computer—is a product of a particular economic and political context and carries with it a program, an agenda, and a philosophy that may or may not be life-enhancing and that therefore requires scrutiny, criticism, and control.[28]

I think it's wise to cultivate a healthy suspicion of technology. Technological, and even economic, progress does not necessarily equal human progress. Just because it's newer and/or faster doesn't mean it's better (as heretical as that sounds). Don't get sucked into the capitalistic marketing ploy. What looks like progression is often regression with an agenda. Others get rich; you get distracted and addicted. As Gandhi wisely said, "There is more to life than increasing its speed."

We idealize the Amish in ways I assume are unhealthy, but it's worth saying they aren't actually against all modern technology. When a new technology comes into society, they evaluate it from the sidelines. They watch us like scientists watch lab rats with a new drug. Does it make us healthier? Or sick? Is it a net positive or no? They let us volunteer for the human trial. Then they have a community-wide conversation. In the case of the car, they decided against it on the grounds that it would destroy their tight-knit community and give life to consumerism, both of which eat away at love, joy, and peace.

To be a fly on the wall when they discussed the smartphone . . .

But the Amish, and other serious followers of Jesus, remind us: There was a time when life was much, *much* slower. There were no cars to drive, planes to catch, all-night study marathons to caffeinate our way through, no constant streams of alerts on our phones, no bottomless holes of entertainment options in our queues.

It's easy to just assume this pace of life is *normal.* It's not. The "time famine" we grew up in is relatively recent. We're still testing it out as a species. And the early results are terrifying.

To summarize: after millennia of slow, gradual acceleration, in recent decades the sheer velocity of our culture has reached an exponential fever pitch.

My question is simple: What is all this distraction, addiction, and pace of life doing to our *souls*?

Something is deeply wrong

The story goes like this: It's the height of British colonialism. An English traveler lands in Africa, intent on a rapid journey into the jungle. He charters some local porters to carry his supplies. After an exhausting day of travel, all on foot, and a fitful night's sleep, he gets up to continue the journey. But the porters refuse. Exasperated, he begins to cajole, bribe, plead, but nothing works. They will not move an inch. Naturally, he asks why.

Answer? They are waiting "for their souls to catch up with their bodies."

Lettie Cowman, in her telling of this story, wrote,

> This whirling rushing life which so many of us live does for us what that first march did for those poor jungle

tribesmen. The difference: *they knew* what they needed to restore life's balance; too often *we do not.*[1]

And it's not just spiritual writers from a century ago who are claiming our life speed is out of control and dangerous. More and more experts are weighing in. Psychologists and mental health professionals are now talking about an epidemic of the modern world: "hurry sickness." As in, they label it a *disease.*

Here's one definition:

A behavior pattern characterized by continual rushing and anxiousness.

Here's another:

A malaise in which a person feels chronically short of time, and so tends to perform every task faster and to get flustered when encountering any kind of delay.[2]

Meyer Friedman—the cardiologist who rose to fame for theorizing that type A people who are chronically angry and in a hurry are more prone to heart attacks—defined it thus:

A continuous struggle and unremitting attempt to accomplish or achieve more and more things or participate in more and more events in less and less time.[3]

Friedman was the one who originally coined the phrase *hurry sickness* after noticing that most of his at-risk cardiovascular patients displayed a harrying "sense of time urgency."[4]

And—deep breath—he said that in the '50s.

Cough, cough.

Awkward silence.

Ahem . . .

How do you know if you have this up-and-coming disease?

It's fairly straightforward. Rosemary Sword and Philip Zimbardo, authors of *The Time Cure,* offer these symptoms of hurry sickness:

- Moving from one check-out line to another because it looks shorter/faster.

- Counting the cars in front of you and either getting in the lane that has the least or is going the fastest.

- Multi-tasking to the point of forgetting one of the tasks.[5]

Anybody?

You feeling this?

Not to play armchair psychologist, but I'm pretty sure we *all* have hurry sickness.

And hurry is a form of violence on the soul.

A lot of you still don't believe me, so let's take a little self-inventory.

Here are my ten symptoms of hurry sickness. Check if the symptom rings true for you:

1. **Irritability**—You get mad, frustrated, or just annoyed *way* too easily. Little, normal things irk you. People have to tiptoe around your ongoing low-grade negativity, if not anger. Word of advice from a fellow eggshell-expert: to self-diagnose don't look at how you treat a colleague or neighbor; look at how you treat those closest to you: your spouse, children, roommate, etc. _____

2. **Hypersensitivity**—All it takes is a minor comment to hurt your feelings, a grumpy email to set you off, or a little turn of events to throw you into an emotional funk and ruin your day. Minor things quickly escalate to major emotional events. Depending on your personality, this might show up as anger or nitpicky-ness or anxiety or depression or just tiredness. Point is, the ordinary problems of life this side of Eden have a disproportionate effect on your emotional well-being and relational grace. You can't seem to roll with the punches. _____

3. **Restlessness**—When you actually do try to slow down and rest, you can't relax. You give Sabbath a try, and you hate it. You read Scripture but find it boring. You have quiet time with God but can't focus your mind. You go to bed early but toss and turn with anxiety. You watch TV but simultaneously check your

phone, fold laundry, and get into a spat on Twitter (okay, maybe you just answer an email). Your mind and body are hyped up on the drug of speed, and when they don't get the next dopamine fix, they shiver. _____

4. **Workaholism (or just nonstop activity)**—You just don't know when to stop. Or worse, you *can't* stop. Another hour, another day, another week. Your drugs of choice are accomplishment and accumulation. These could show up as careerism or just as obsessive housecleaning and errand running. Result: you fall prey to "sunset fatigue," where by day's end you have nothing left to give to your spouse, children, or loved ones. They get the grouchy, curt, overtired you, and it's not pretty. _____

5. **Emotional numbness**—You just don't have the capacity to *feel* another's pain. Or your own pain for that matter. Empathy is a rare feeling for you. You just don't have the time for it. You live in this kind of constant fugue. _____

6. **Out-of-order priorities**—You feel disconnected from your identity and calling. You're always getting sucked into the tyranny of the urgent, not the important. Your life is reactive, not proactive. You're busier than ever before yet still feel like you don't have time for what really matters to you. Months often go by or *years*—or, God forbid, maybe it's been *decades*—and you realize you still haven't gotten around to all the things you *said* were the most important in your life. _____

7. **Lack of care for your body**—You don't have time for the basics: eight hours of sleep a night; daily exercise; healthy, home-cooked food; minimal stimulants; margin. You gain weight. Get sick multiple times a year. Regularly wake up tired. Don't sleep well. Live off the four horsemen of the industrialized food apocalypse: caffeine, sugar, processed carbs, and alcohol. _____

8. **Escapist behaviors**—When we're too tired to do what's actually life giving for our souls, we each turn to our distraction of choice: overeating, overdrinking, binge-watching Netflix, browsing social media, surfing the web, looking at porn—name your preferred cultural narcotic. Narcotics are good, healthy even, on an occasional and short-term basis when they shield us from unnecessary pain; but when we abuse them to escape from reality, they eat us alive. You find yourself stuck in the negative feedback loop of socially acceptable addictions. _____

9. **Slippage of spiritual disciplines**—If you're anything like me, when you get overbusy, the things that are truly life giving for your soul are the first to go rather than your first *go to*—such as a quiet time in the morning, Scripture, prayer, Sabbath, worship on Sunday, a meal with your community, and so on. Because in an ironic catch-22, the things that make for rest actually take a bit of emotional energy and self-discipline. When we get overbusy, we get overtired, and when we get overtired, we don't have the energy or discipline to do what we need most for our souls. Repeat. The cycle begins to feed off its

own energy. So instead of life with God, we settle for life with a Netflix subscription and a glass of cheap red wine. A very poor substitute. Not because time wasted on TV is the great Satan but because we rarely get done binge-watching *anything* (or posting to social media, or overeating Five Guys burgers and fries, etc.) and feel awake and alive from the soul outward, rested, refreshed, and ready for a new day. We delay the inevitable: an emotional crash. And as a consequence, we miss out on the life-giving sense of the with-ness of God. _____

10. **Isolation**—You feel disconnected from God, others, and your own soul. On those rare times when you actually stop to pray (and by pray I don't mean ask God for stuff; I mean sit with God in the quiet), you're so stressed and distracted that your mind can't settle down long enough to enjoy the Father's company. Same with your friends: when you're with them, you're also with your phone or a million miles away in your mind, running down the to-do list. And even when you're alone, you come face to face with the void that is your soul and immediately run back to the familiar groove of busyness and digital distraction.[6] _____

Okay, do the math . . .

How did you score?

Seven out of ten?

Eight?

Yeah, don't worry; you're not alone.[7]

Reject any guilt or shame you're feeling right now. It's not helpful, rarely from God, and definitely not my agenda with this little exercise.

The point I'm driving toward is this: an overbusy, hurried life of speed is the new normal in the Western world, and it's *toxic*. Psychologists tell us anxiety is often the canary in the coal mine, our souls' way of telling us something is deeply wrong and we need to fix it, fast. In one recent study 39 percent of Americans reported being more anxious than they were a year ago.[8] That's not something to keep your eye on; it's an emotional epidemic. As my grandma used to say, "Just because everybody's doing it, don't make it smart."

And as I said before: hurry is a threat not only to our emotional health but to our spiritual lives as well.

Thomas Merton once called "the rush and pressure of modern life" a "pervasive form of contemporary violence."[9] *Violence* is the perfect word.

Hurry kills relationships. Love takes time; hurry doesn't have it.

It kills joy, gratitude, appreciation; people in a rush don't have time to enter the goodness of the moment.

It kills wisdom; wisdom is born in the quiet, the slow. Wisdom has its own pace. It makes you wait for it—wait for the inner voice to come to the surface of your tempestuous mind, but not until waters of thought settle and calm.

Hurry kills all that we hold dear: spirituality, health, marriage, family, thoughtful work, creativity, generosity . . . name your value. Hurry is a sociopathic predator loose in our society.

In his moving book on the Sabbath, Wayne Muller observed:

> A "successful" life has become a violent enterprise. We make war on our own bodies, pushing them beyond their limits; war on our children, because we cannot find enough time to be with them when they are hurt and afraid, and need our company; war on our spirit, because we are too preoccupied to listen to the quiet voices that seek to nourish and refresh us; war on our communities, because we are fearfully protecting what we have, and do not feel safe enough to be kind and generous; war on the earth, because we cannot take the time to place our feet on the ground and allow it to feed us, to taste its blessings and give thanks.[10]

The poet Mary Oliver, not a Christian but a lifelong spiritual seeker, wrote something similar: "Attention is the beginning of devotion."[11] Worship and joy start with the capacity to turn our minds' attention toward the God who is always with us in the now. As apprentices of Jesus, this is our main task *and* the locus of the devil's stratagem against us. Many have noted that the modern world is a virtual conspiracy against the interior life. It's hard not to see a darker force behind all this than simple capitalism. When we uncritically hurry our way through our digital terrain, we make the devil's job relatively easy. Regardless of our income levels, attention is our scarcest resource. Jesus wisely said our hearts will follow behind our treasures.[12] Usually we interpret *treasure* to mean our two basic resources: time and money. But an even more precious resource is attention. Without it our spiritual lives are stillborn in the womb.

Because *attention* leads to *awareness.* All the contemplatives agree. The mystics point out that what's missing is awareness. Meaning, in the chronic problem of human beings' felt experience of distance from God, God isn't usually the culprit. God is omnipresent—there is no place God is not. And no time he isn't present either. Our *awareness* of God is the problem, and it's acute.

So many people live without a sense of God's presence through the day. We talk about his absence as if it's this great question of theodicy. And I get that: I've been through the dark night of the soul. But could it be that, with a few said exceptions, we're the ones who are absent, not God? We sit around sucked into our phones or TV or to-do lists, oblivious to the God who is around us, with us, *in us,* even more desirous than we are for relationship.

This is why I harp on technology. At the risk of sounding like an overzealous cult leader with spittle on his beard or a fundie Luddite with an ax to grind, I fear for the future of the church. There is more at stake here than our attentions spans.

Because *what you give your attention to is the person you become.*

Put another way: the mind is the portal to the soul, and what you fill your mind with will shape the trajectory of your character. In the end, your life is no more than the sum of what you gave your attention to. That bodes well for those apprentices of Jesus who give the bulk of their attention to him and to all that is good, beautiful, and true in his world. But not for those who give their attention to the 24-7 news cycle of outrage and anxiety and emotion-charged drama or the nonstop feed of celebrity gossip, titillation, and cultural drivel. (As if we "give" it in the first place; much of it is stolen by a clever algorithm out to monetize our precious attention.)

But again: we become what we give our attention to, for better or worse.

Some of the most sincere and honest people I know tell me that when they get into the presence of God, they just can't pay attention. And if we lose our capacity to pay attention to God—for long, or even short, lengths of time—who knows who we'll become?

You see, not only is hurry toxic to our emotional health and spiritual lives, but it's also symptomatic of much deeper issues of the heart.

I love how John Ortberg framed it: "Hurry is not just a disordered schedule. Hurry is a disordered heart."[13]

All too often our hurry is a sign of something else. Something deeper. Usually that we're running away from something— father wounds, childhood trauma, last names, deep insecurity or deficits of self-worth, fear of failure, pathological inability to accept the limitations of our humanity, or simply boredom with the mundanity of middle life.

Or we're running *to* something—promotions or purchases or experiences or stamps on our passports or the next high—searching in vain for something no earthly experience has on offer: a sense of self-worth and love and acceptance. In the meritocracy of the West, it's easy to feel like we're only as good as our next sales commissions or quarterly reports or music singles or *sermons* or Instagram posts or new toys. So we're constantly out of breath, chasing the ever-elusive wind.

Sometimes our hurry is less dramatic: we're just overbusy, more victims of the rights and responsibilities of the modern world than perpetrators of escapism. But either way, the effect is the same. It's what William Irvine called "misliving." In his book *A Guide to the Good Life,* he wrote:

> There is a danger that you will mislive—that despite all your activity, despite all the pleasant diversions you might have enjoyed while alive, you will end up living a bad life. There is, in other words, a danger that when you are on your deathbed, you will look back and realize that you wasted your one chance at living. Instead of spending your life pursuing something genuinely valuable, you squandered it because you allowed yourself to be distracted by the various baubles life has to offer.[14]

Cue the haunting line from Jesus of Nazareth: "What good is it for someone to gain the whole world, yet forfeit their soul?"[15]

Have you lost your soul?

Or at least part of it?

Want to get it back?

Keep reading.

Part two:

The solution

Hint: the solution isn't more time

So.

We have a problem.

Time.

But here's the thing—and please listen carefully—the solution is *not* more time.

On a regular basis I catch myself saying, "I wish there were ten more hours in a day." Even as I mouth it, I realize my logic is flawed. Think about it: even if God were a Robin Williams-esque genie in a bottle, there to make my every wish come true, and he were to alter the structure of the universe to give me ten more hours in a day, what would I likely do with those ten hours? The same thing most people would do—fill them up with even *more* things, and then I would be even *more* tired and burned out and emotionally frayed and spiritually at risk than I am now.

Don't get me wrong; I'd fill them up with good things, even great things. I'd pick up music again, master the Sonata Pathétique on piano, start a band. Read *Anna Karenina*. Then David Foster Wallace's entire library. Volunteer at my kids' school and our church's daily feeding program for houseless people. Practice more hospitality with neighbors. Spend more time with my kids. Become a chef—yes, definitely that. Then join CrossFit. Flat abs *and* tapas. Travel, especially to places where I can display said abs. Go back to school. Finally finish *The West Wing* (I dropped off in season 5). Write poetry. I'd . . . oh wait, I think I've used up my extra ten hours and then some. Same problem *again*.

What would you do? Go BASE jumping? Knit a winter coat? Start a nonprofit? Whatever you did, you'd likely end up just like me—even more exhausted than you are now.

Here's my point: the solution to an overbusy life is *not* more time.

It's to slow down and simplify our lives around what really matters.

You have all sorts of sharp, secular thinkers like Greg McKeown and Joshua Fields Millburn writing about essentialism and minimalism, which is great. I eat those books up.[1] But these ideas are what followers of Jesus have been saying for *millennia*. We'll get to the intersection of hurry and the way of

Jesus in a few pages, but for now think about *Genesis,* the opening book in the library of Scripture. Our defining narrative says that we're made "in the image of God,"[2] but also: we're made "from the dust."[3]

Image and dust.

To be made in the image of God means that we're rife with potential. We have the Divine's capacity in our DNA. We're *like* God. We were created to "imago" his behavior, to *rule* like he does, to gather up the raw materials of our planet and reshape them into a world for human beings to flourish and thrive.

But that's only half the story.

We're also made from the dirt, "ashes to ashes, dust to dust": we're the original biodegradable containers. Which means we're born with limitations. We're not God. We're mortal, not immortal. Finite, not infinite.

Image and dust.

Potential and limitations.

One of the key tasks of our apprenticeship to Jesus is living into both our potential *and* our limitations.

There's a lot of talk right now about reaching your full potential, and I'm all for it. Step out. Risk it all. Have faith. Chase the dream God put in your heart. Become the Technicolor version of who you were made to be.

But again, that's only half the story.

What you hear very little of—inside *or* outside the church—is accepting your limitations.

Doesn't really have the ring of a *New York Times* bestseller, does it? *Accepting Your Limitations: How to Make Peace with Your Mortality and Cosmic Insignificance.* Yeah, as great as my publisher is, I doubt they would go for that.[4]

We live in a culture that wants to transgress all limitations, not accept them—to cheat time and space. To "be like God."[5] To watch every new film, listen to every podcast, read every new book (and don't forget the classics!), hear every record, go to every concert, drive every road trip, travel to every country (another stamp for the passport, *please*), eat at every new restaurant, party at every new bar opening, befriend every new face, fix every problem in society, rise to the top of every field, win every award, make every list of who's who—

#YOLO.

#FOMO.

#imsostressedouticantbreathe.

Have you heard people talk about "entertainment anxiety" yet? I love this idea. We're to the point now where there's so much good TV and film and art out there to consume that whenever somebody asks me, "Have you watched _____?" I immediately feel a rush of anxiety: *Oh no, seriously? Another TV show to add to my queue?* As I said, I'm already three seasons behind on *The West Wing* (where was I in the late '90s?!), and now I find out there's some indie British show called *The Night Manager* that, apparently, I just *have* to see if I want to even stand a chance at being cool and cultured.

There goes another twenty hours I don't have. Dahhh . . . .

Listen, I have good news for you. Great news, in fact.

You.

Can't.

Do.

It.

All.

And neither can I.

We're *human.* Time, space, one place at a time, all that pesky non-omnipresent stuff.

We have limitations. Lots of them. The limitations include but are not, well, limited to these:

1. Our bodies. As I said, unlike Luke Skywalker, we can be in only one place at a time. Hence the rub on limitations.

2. Our minds. We can only "know in part,"[6] as Paul once said, and the problem is, we don't know what

we don't know. Nobody is an encyclopedia. We all miss things. As the saying goes, "My people are destroyed from lack of knowledge."[7] What we don't know often can and will hurt us. Our IQs, which are *not* the same across the board, also limit us. Yes, the mind is much like a muscle, and we can exercise it to its full potential. But no matter how much I read or study or how many degrees I pursue, I will simply never have the intelligence of many of the people I most look up to. This is a fairly significant limitation.

3. Our giftings. On a similar note as above, I will simply never have the giftings of many of the people I most look up to. Comparison just eats away at our joy, doesn't it? Whatever your thing is—parenting, painting, music, entrepreneurship, origami—whatever—there will *always* be somebody better at it than you. Always. Stings, doesn't it? But why should it? What is it about the human condition that makes it well-nigh impossible for many of us to celebrate both those who are more gifted than we are *and* our own best work? When did the standard for success become a celebrity's magnum opus, not our own sweat and tears?

4. Our personalities and emotional wiring. We have only so much capacity. I'm an introvert. I'm actually deeply relational, but my relational plate is small. I'm also melancholy by nature. I hate to admit it, but some people have a *lot* more capacity than I do. They can relate to more people, carry more responsibility, handle more stress, work more hours, lead more people, and so on, than I could ever dream of. Even the best version of me can't do it all.

5. Our families of origin. None of us start with a blank slate. Some of us start with a leg up in life. Others of us walk with a limp from our early years. A mother wound. An absent father. Nominal or nonexistent faith in our parents. Generational poverty. Our families set some limits on our lives before we even come out of the womb.

6. Our socioeconomic origins. America is built around the myth of a classless society. A myth that conceals a deep well of injustice. The truth is, even in our land of opportunity, some people just have more opportunity than others. One of the great tragedies of America is that privilege is all too often (if not usually) connected to the color of your skin. If you're like me—white, male, middle class—you realize after a while that you started the game from third base; some of your friends started in the parking lot. The game was rigged in your favor. But no matter how high up the Western social hierarchy you started, there's *always* somebody above you. Always.

7. Our education and careers. If you dropped out of high school, that's a limitation. If you have a PhD from Harvard, that's another, in an odd way. Your career might limit you because it's low paying or hard on your body's energy reserves *or* because you're so successful that you have to work insane hours just to stay on top of the load.

8. Our seasons of life and their responsibilities—like going to college or raising a young child or caring for dying parents. In some seasons we just have very little extra time to give away. Many have noted that

most of us are money-poor when we're young, but we have time. Especially when we're single. But as we age and pick the constraints that define our lives, it flips: many of us now have money but are time-poor. I'm nearing forty; I own a home, have money to occasionally eat out, even vacation in Kauai every few years—things my twenty-year-old self would have only dreamed of. Yet I have just shy of zero free time. Between my work as a pastor and my (even more important) work as a husband and father, my days are jammed full. Family is a limitation. I've thought about renaming my kids Limitation 1, Limitation 2, and Limitation 3 . . . They cost me, and this is true of any relationship you have but especially of your relationship with your kids—an enormous amount of time, energy, and attention. This isn't bad; it's wonderful. But it's a limitation for this season, one that is over two decades long.

9. Our eighty or so years of life, if we're that blessed. There's no guarantee. But whether we live to 18 or 108, life is fleeting. One New Testament writer called it "a wisp."[8] There's simply no way to do it all, at least not this time around.

10. God's call on our lives. I hesitate to say this because it would be easy to misinterpret, but there are limits to God's call on each of us. I think of Peter's envy of John's call over his own less-pleasant assignment of an upside-down crucifixion. Jesus had to lovingly reprimand Peter: "What is that to you? You must follow me."[9] Many of us need to hear those same words and find freedom in them.

Is this list exhaustive? Of course not. It's only a sampling. My point is, our limitations aren't just temporal but emotional, social, economic, and more.

What if these limitations aren't something to fight but to gratefully accept as a signpost to God's call on our souls? I love Peter Scazzero's line: "We find God's will for our lives in our limitations."[10]

Don't misread me: *the same is true* for our potential. My language here could easily be manipulated or misinterpreted to say something that is at best un-American and at worst unjust.

But I doubt Jesus' agenda is to make poor people middle class or middle-class people wealthy. Jesus blessed the "poor in spirit"[11] by the thousands, gave them the Sermon on the Mount,[12] and then sent them home, *still poor,* but blessed. Jesus' agenda is to make wounded people *whole.* That often leads to more money or opportunity or influence, and I'm all for it. After all, we were created to rule over the earth; nothing brings me more joy than to see men and women take their rightful place as loving, wise, creative, powerful rulers in society.

All I'm saying is limitations aren't all bad. They are where we find God's will for our lives.

And the main limitation we all share—regardless of where you started in life or how smart or hard working or type A you are—is time. It doesn't matter if you're the CEO of a multi-national corporation or a retired school bus driver, if you're single or raising a family of seven, if you live in the wind tunnel of a global city or on a farm in the middle of Kansas without cell service or Wi-Fi. *Nobody* has more than twenty-four hours in a day.

We simply can't see, read, watch, taste, drink, experience, be, or do it all. Not an option.

Life is a series of choices. Every yes is a thousand nos. Every activity we give our time to is a thousand other activities we *can't* give our time to. Because, duh: we can't be in two places at once.

We have to learn to say no. *Constantly.* As Anne Lamott so humorously pointed out, " 'No' is a complete sentence."[13] And it's one we need to work into our vocabulary.

In the language of Henry David Thoreau, we have to "live deliberately." I just finished reading his famous memoir, *Walden,* about going into the woods for two full years to slow down and simplify. Take a look at this line:

> I went to the woods because I wished to live deliberately, to front only the essential facts of life, and see if I could not learn what it had to teach, and not, when I came to die, discover that I had not lived.[14]

Do you ever catch yourself with the sneaking suspicion that you'll wake up on your deathbed with this nagging sense that somehow, in all the hurry and busyness and frenetic activity, you missed the most important things?

Somehow you started a business but ended a marriage.

You got your kids to their dream colleges but never taught them the way of Jesus.

You got letters after your name but learned the hard way that intelligence is not the same as wisdom.

You made a lot of money but never grew rich in the things that matter most. Which, ironically, aren't things at all.

You watched all fourteen seasons of _____ but never learned to love prayer.

This is the terrifying aspect of this conversation for me; most of us waste copious amounts of time. Myself included. For all the talk about hurry and overload, most of it is self-inflicted. Philip Zimbardo's recent research on the "Demise of Guys" (i.e., the crisis of masculinity in Western culture) has concluded the average guy spends ten thousand hours playing video games by age twenty-one.[15]

Ten thousand hours.

My mind jumps to the research around this rule; in ten thousand hours, you could master any craft or become an expert in any field—from Sumerian archeology to Olympic water polo. You could get your bachelor's degree *and* your master's degree. You could memorize the New Testament.

Or, you could beat level four of *Call of Duty.*

And how we spend our time is how we spend our *lives.* It's who we become (or don't become).

Apparently, I'm known as a "reader." I read two or three books a week, which normally comes in at around one hundred and twenty-five books a year. And I feel pretty good about that. At least I did. Until I read Charles Chu's calculations. The average American reads two hundred to four hundred words per minute. At that speed we could all read *two hundred* books a year, nearly twice my quota, in just 417 hours.

Sounds like a lot, right? 417? That's over an hour a day.

But can you guess how much time the average American spends on social media each year? The number is 705 hours.

TV . . . *2,737.5* hours.

Meaning, for just a fraction of the time we give to social media and television, we could *all* become avid readers to the nth degree. Chu lamented:

> Here's the simple truth behind reading a lot of books. It's not that hard. We have all the time we need. The scary part—the part we all ignore—is that we are too addicted, too weak, and too distracted to do what we all know is important.[16]

If this is true of *reading,* how much more is it true of our lives with God?

What else could we give thousands of hours of our year to?

In twenty minutes of *Candy Crush* on our morning bus ride, we could pray for every single one of our friends and family members.

In an hour of TV before bed, we could read through the entire Bible. In six months.

In a day running errands and shopping for crap we really don't need, we could practice Sabbath—an entire seventh of our lives devoted to rest, worship, and the celebration of our journey through God's good world.

You see what I'm getting at?

Long before Thoreau went off into the woods, Paul said:

> Look carefully then how you walk, not as unwise but as wise, making the best use of the time, because the days are evil.[17]

That next to last phrase can be translated from the Greek in a few ways:

- Redeeming the time

- Making the most of every opportunity

- Make the most of every chance you get[18]

Every day is a chance. Every hour an opportunity. Every moment a precious gift.

How will you spend yours? Will you squander them on trivial things? Or invest them in the eternal kind of life?

Of course, most of us *want* to spend our time wisely. But many of us are not single like Paul, or we're not an independently wealthy bachelor like Thoreau. We hate how addictive we are, how easily distracted we've become.

So maybe better questions are, How do we "live deliberately" *without* going off into the forest to scavenge our own food or abandoning our family? How do we slow down, simplify, and live deliberately *right in the middle* of the chaos of the noisy, fast-paced, urban, digital world we call home?

Well, the answer, of course, is easy: follow Jesus.

The secret of the easy yoke

And now for the question you've all been asking: What does any of this have to do with following Jesus?

That is, after all, kind of my gig. I'm a pastor and a teacher of the way of Jesus, not a therapist, self-help guru, or time-management consultant. Sadly. Motivational speaker does have a nice ring to it. But I'm more likely to say, "Turn in your Bibles to . . ." than offer a tip or technique on how to make your small-business dream come true or lay out a protein-to-carbs ratio to revolutionize your morning routine. If only.

But I'm guessing you're reading this book not *just* because you feel hurried but because to some degree you find the life of Jesus compelling.

(That, or you're single and you find the boy or girl who gave you this book compelling. Either way, I'm happy you've come along for the ride.)

Were I a betting man, I'd also wager that before I said a word, you were already smart enough to intuit some kind of a correlation between hurry and spirituality. I've just put language, history, and data to what you already know: we have a problem with hurry. If you're still reading this, it's either because you're the kind of person who has to finish every book you start (we share the same psychosis) or because you still have enough faith in me that you're optimistic a solution is en route.

Let me show you what the way of Jesus has to say to the epidemic of hurry.

To start, Jesus was a rabbi. (Hebrew, meaning "teacher.") Yes, he was more—the Messiah and the embodiment of God himself. I deeply believe that. But if you had been a first-century Jew and Jesus showed up in your synagogue one Sabbath morning, the odds are, the category you would have put him in was that of a rabbi or a traveling sage.

And like every rabbi in his day, Jesus had two things.

First, he had a yoke. Not a literal yoke; he was a teacher, not a farmer. A yoke was a common idiom in the first century for a rabbi's way of reading the Torah. But it was also more: it was his set of teachings on how to be human. His way to shoulder the (at times crippling) weight of life—marriage, divorce, prayer, money, sex, conflict resolution, government—all of it. It's an odd image for those of us who don't live in an agrarian society. But imagine two oxen yoked together to pull a cart or plow a field. A yoke is how you shoulder a load.

What made Jesus unique wasn't that he had a yoke; all rabbis had a yoke. It was that he had an *easy* yoke.

Secondly, Jesus had apprentices. In Hebrew the word is *talmidim.* It's usually translated as "disciples," and that's just fine, but I think an even better word to capture the idea behind *talmidim* is "apprentices."

To be one of Jesus' *talmidim* is to apprentice under Jesus. Put simply, it's to organize your life around three basic goals:

1. Be with Jesus.

2. Become like Jesus.

3. Do what he would do if he were you.

The whole point of apprenticeship is to model *all* of your life after Jesus. And in doing so to recover your soul. To have the warped part of you put back into shape. To experience healing in the deepest parts of your being. To experience what Jesus called "life . . . to the full."[1] What the New Testament writers call "salvation."[2] Keep in mind, the Greek word that we translate "salvation" is *soteria;* it's the same word we translate "healing." When you're reading the New Testament and you read that somebody was "healed" by Jesus and then you read somebody else was "saved" by Jesus, *you're reading the same Greek word.* Salvation *is* healing. Even the etymology of our English word *salvation* comes from the Latin *salve.* As in, an ointment you put on a burn or a wound.

This is what Jesus was all about—healing people, saving them, at a soul-deep level.

How? Through apprenticeship to him.

So everywhere Jesus went, he was constantly offering an invitation.

Usually it sounded like this:

> Come, follow me.[3]

Or like this:

> Come, be my apprentice.

That was Jesus' go-to language for people to come and find healing in apprenticeship to him. And I love it. But let's come back to *another* invitation of Jesus. The one we started this book off with, from Matthew 11. It doesn't get as much airplay, but it's my favorite by far. Do me a favor: reread it, but this time slowly, giving each word time to metabolize into your system:

> Come to me, all you who are weary and burdened, and I will give you rest. Take my yoke upon you and learn from me, for I am gentle and humble in heart, and you will find rest for your souls. For my yoke is easy and my burden is light.[4]

Okay, let's read it one *more* time. Even slower. Breathe deeply; don't rush this part; God has something for you in this moment:

Come to me, all you who are weary and burdened . . .
And I will give you rest.
Take my yoke upon you and learn from me . . .
For I am gentle and humble in heart . . .
And you will find rest for your souls.
For my yoke is easy . . .
And my burden is light.

Now read Eugene Peterson's paraphrase of those same verses in The Message. Again, slowly:

Are you tired? Worn out? Burned out on religion? Come to me. Get away with me and you'll recover your life. I'll show you how to take a real rest. Walk with me and work with me—watch how I do it. Learn the unforced rhythms of grace. I won't lay anything heavy or ill-fitting on you. Keep company with me and you'll learn to live freely and lightly.

"Learn the unforced rhythms of grace." How good is that line?

This is an *invitation*—for all the tired, the burned out, the stressed, and all those stuck in traffic and behind on their to-do lists, reaching for *another* cup of coffee just to make it through the day.

Anybody like that out there?

Let me rephrase the question: Anybody *not* like that out there?

In her BuzzFeed article "How Millennials Became the Burnout

Generation," Anne Petersen commented that "burnout isn't a place to visit and come back from; it's our permanent residence." What used to be the isolated experience of a New York day trader or emergency room physician is now the reality for *most* people. Petersen offered an erudite critique of the $11 billion self-actualization industry and the inability of a spa day to fix our problems with burnout. Yet after a lengthy diagnosis of our generation's ennui, the only attempt at a solution she had to offer is "democratic socialism and . . . unions. We are beginning to understand what ails us, and it's not something an oxygen facial or a treadmill desk can fix."**5**

I've nothing against unions, and I'm fine with democratic socialism (don't judge me—Portland, remember?). But I highly doubt they will be any more effective against burnout than essential oils.

Jesus's invitation is to take up his yoke—to travel through life at his side, learning from him how to shoulder the weight of life with ease. To step out of the burnout society to a life of soul rest.

Now, this sounds great, but let me call out the elephant in the room: how many of you read this invitation of Jesus and think . . .

I think I'm a follower of Jesus, as far as I can tell.

But honestly, I am tired.

I am worn out. I live with a low-grade fatigue that rarely goes away.

And honestly? I am a little burned out on religion.

What gives? Am I missing something?

It took me a lot of years—many of them tough sledding—to figure out, *yes,* I *am* missing something. Something that was staring me in the face for most of my life.

Now, listen carefully: if you grew up in the church, the odds are high that you know this verse in *Matthew* very well. It's reached cliche status in some circles. I grew up in the '80s (it wasn't nearly as cool as *Stranger Things* makes it look), back when Christian grandmothers would cross-stitch Bible verses and then frame them on the bathroom wall, to the right of the soap. Anybody know what I'm talking about? Yeah . . . This verse was a favorite of grandmas across the Western world. And the danger with that is it's easy to grow numb or even blind to what's embedded in this verse.

Hidden in plain sight in this invitation of Jesus is what Dallas Willard called "the secret of the easy yoke."

He wrote this about Matthew 11:

> In this truth lies the secret of the easy yoke: the secret involves living as [Jesus] lived in the entirety of his life—adopting his overall life-style. . . .
>
> Our mistake is to think that following Jesus consists in loving our enemies, going the "second mile," turning the other cheek, suffering patiently and hopefully—while living the rest of our lives just as everyone else around us does. . . . It's a strategy bound to fail.[6]

What he's saying here is simple but profound.

Here's my paraphrase of the secret of the easy yoke:

> If you want to experience the *life* of Jesus, you have to adopt the *lifestyle* of Jesus.

As long as I'm repeating things, one more time:

If you want to experience the *life* of Jesus, you have to adopt the *lifestyle* of Jesus.

When this clicked for me, it changed everything. To break it down, a quick story.

I live right on the edge of downtown Portland in this fun micro-urban neighborhood. Across the street is a house full of single people who are essentially a walking advertisement for Nike. Nike is based in Portland's suburbs, and I'm not sure if they work for the swoosh, or are sponsored, or what, but all six of them are avid runners. Now, I run, but I'm not a *runner*. You know what I mean? These people are runners.

And frequently, early in the morning as I'm sitting there drinking my coffee and praying, I see them file out the front door to go for a sunrise run. Naturally, they are all wearing tights, and trust me, they look *good*. Single-digit body fat. That lean-but-muscular look. Impeccable posture: shoulders back, chin up. And then, they start to prance . . . I mean, run. They look more antelope than human. Seriously, their warm-up is faster than my speed workout. (Granted, my speed workout is in need of a pick-me-up, but still.)

And regularly as they run off, I think to myself, *I want that.* I want to look good in spandex. (Sadly, *Runner's World* still hasn't called for a photo shoot.) I want to run a six-minute mile without breaking a sweat. I want that level of health and energy and vitality.

I want that life.

But then I think about the lifestyle behind it.

While I was up watching *The Man in the High Castle* and drinking red wine until midnight (hypothetical scenario, I promise . . .), they ate celery and water for dinner and went to bed at 9 p.m.

While I was sipping my Kenyan single origin in my bathrobe, they were out sweating through the humid goop of summer and ice of winter.

When I run, I catch up on a podcast or stare off into space thinking about my teaching for Sunday; they run intervals every four hundred meters and stretch their lungs to the breaking point.

I run a cost-benefit analysis and quickly decide, as great as their tights look in the morning fog, it's not worth the pain. So I simply spectate.

The reality is, *I want the life, but I'm not willing to adopt the lifestyle behind it.*

I think that's how a lot of us feel about Jesus.

We read the stories of Jesus—his joy, his resolute peace through uncertainty, his unanxious presence, his relaxed manner and how in the moment he was—and think, *I want that life.* We hear his open invite to "life . . . to the full" and think, *Sign me up.* We hear about his easy yoke and soul-deep rest and think, *Gosh, yes,* heck *yes. I* need *that.* But then we're not willing to adopt his lifestyle.

But in Jesus' case it is worth the cost. In fact, you get back far more than you give up. There's a cross, yes, a death, but it's followed by an empty tomb, a new portal to life. Because in the way of Jesus, death is *always* followed by resurrection.

Here's a conviction of mine: the Western church has lost sight of the fact that the way of Jesus is just that: a *way* of life. It's not just a set of ideas (what we call *theology*) or a list of dos and don'ts (what we call *ethics*). I mean, it is that, but it's so much more. It's a way of life based on that of Jesus himself. A lifestyle.

The church tradition I grew up in made much of theology and ethics; but little to nothing was said about lifestyle. But lifestyle is where the money is.

As long as we're riffing on Eugene Peterson, he once wrote this about Jesus' metaphor of the way:

> The Jesus way wedded to the Jesus truth brings about the Jesus life. . . .
> But Jesus as the truth gets far more attention than Jesus as the way. Jesus as the way is the most frequently evaded metaphor among the Christians with

whom I have worked for fifty years as a North American pastor.[7]

Apparently, my church wasn't the only one to de-emphasize the way of Jesus as a lifestyle. What a tragic misstep.

Your life is the by-product of your lifestyle. By *life* I mean your experience of the human condition, and by *lifestyle* I mean the rhythms and routines that make up your day-to-day existence. The way you organize your time. Spend your money.

There's a saying in business literature that I love: "Every system is perfectly designed to get the results it gets." Usually this is applied to widgets and the bottom line, but I love it for life as a whole.

If the results you are getting are lousy—anxiety at a simmer, mild depression, high levels of stress, chronic emotional burnout, little to no sense of the presence of God, an inability to focus your mind on the things that make for life, etc.—then the odds are very good that something about the system that is your life is off kilter. The way you've organized your morning (or evening) routine, your schedule, your budget, your relationship to your phone; how you manage your resources of time, money, and attention, etc.—*something* is out of whack.

It's often quoted that "the definition of *insanity* is doing the same thing over and over again and expecting different results." But that's *exactly* what we do. We get a vision of the kind of life that is possible in Jesus; we go to church or read a book or listen to a podcast; we catch a glimpse of the kind of life we ache for—one of emotional health and spiritual life. Our gut immediately says, *Yes. God, I want that life.* We head home from church with all the willpower we can muster and set out to change. But then *we go right back to living the exact same lifestyle.* And nothing changes. It's the same cycle on repeat: stress, tiredness, distraction. We feel stuck yet again. And then we wonder, *What am I missing?*

This method of change simply does not work.

What does? Honestly, the solution is very, very simple. If you want to experience the life "to the full" of Jesus, his nonstop, conscious enjoyment of God's presence and world, all you have to do is adopt not only his theology and ethics *but also his lifestyle.* Just follow his way.

That's it!

Just take his life as a template for your own. Take on his habits and practices. As an apprentice, copy your Rabbi's every move. After all, that's the whole point of apprenticeship.

That's what Jesus is getting at with this odd imagery of a yoke, which, when you think about it, is bizarre language for an invitation to "find rest for your souls." I mean, yokes are for farming. Farming is work, not rest.

Frederick Dale Bruner is a top scholar on the gospel of Matthew, and his insight into the paradox of an "easy yoke" is worth reading:

> A yoke is a work instrument. Thus when Jesus offers a

yoke he offers what we might think tired workers need least. They need a mattress or a vacation, not a yoke.

I hope you're laughing right now; that's so insightful and true.

But Jesus realizes that the most restful gift he can give the tired is a new way to carry life, a fresh way to bear responsibilities. . . . Realism sees that life is a succession of burdens; we cannot get away from them; thus instead of offering escape, Jesus offers equipment. Jesus means that obedience to his Sermon on the Mount [his yoke] will develop in us a balance and a "way" of carrying life that will give more rest than the way we have been living.[8]

You see the genius of Jesus' invitation?

There is an emotional and even spiritual weight to life; we *all* feel it, especially as we age. An easy life is a myth, if not a red herring—the by-product of an advertising-drenched and social media–duped culture. Life is hard. Full stop. No comma, no *but,* no endnote. All the wise men and women of history have said as much; no new technology or substance or pill will ever erase humanity's fall. Best-case scenario, we mitigate its effects as we advance Jesus' return. But there's no escaping the pain.

Why do you think there's so much addiction in our world? Not just substance abuse but the more run-of-the-mill addictions to porn or sex or eating or dieting or exercise or work or travel or shopping or social media or even church?

And yes, even church can be an addiction, a dopamine hit

you run toward to escape a father wound or emotional pain or an unhappy marriage . . . but that's another book.

People all over the world—outside the church and in—are looking for an escape, a way out from under the crushing weight to life this side of Eden. But there is no escaping it. The best the world can offer is a temporary distraction to delay the inevitable or deny the inescapable.

That's why Jesus doesn't offer us an escape. He offers us something far better: "equipment." He offers his apprentices a whole new way to bear the weight of our humanity: with ease. At his side. Like two oxen in a field, tied shoulder to shoulder. With Jesus doing all the heavy lifting. At his pace. Slow, unhurried, present to the moment, full of love and joy and peace.

An easy life isn't an option; an easy yoke is.[9]

What we're really talking about is a rule of life

If there's anything you pick up from reading the four Gospels, it's that Jesus was rarely in a hurry.

Can you imagine a stressed-out Jesus? Snapping at Mary Magdalene after a long day, "I can't believe you dropped the hummus." Sighing, and saying to himself, "I seriously need a glass of wine."

Can you picture him half talking to you, half texting on his iPhone, the sporadic "Uh-huh" punctuating a one-sided conversation?

Can you hear him saying, "I'm sorry, I'd love to heal your leg, but I have a plane to catch. I'm speaking at TEDx in Jerusalem tomorrow. Here's Thaddaeus, an apprentice of mine nobody's ever heard of. He's happy to pray for you. I'm out."

Or: "Talk to my assistant, Judas. We'll see if we can squeeze you in."

Or: "What magazine are you with?" You say, "None." His eyes glaze over . . .

Um, *no.*

There's this one story where Jesus' friend Lazarus was sick. By friend, I mean close friend. And by sick, I mean about to die sick. But when Jesus got the life-or-death message, we read this odd line:

> When he heard that Lazarus was sick, he stayed where he was two more days, and then he said to his disciples, "Let us go back to Judea."[1]

Not exactly in a hurry, was he? And his friend's life hung in the balance.

In another story, Jesus was teaching in a synagogue when this guy Jairus literally fell at Jesus' feet, begging him to come and heal his little girl who was "at the point of death."[2] Again, life or death. But on the way to Jairus's home, a woman with a chronic health condition that went back twelve years interrupted Jesus. There's a beautiful story[3] where Jesus just took all the time in the world with her. No rush at all.

Can you imagine how Jairus must have felt? I imagine him tapping his foot, giving Jesus the *Come on!* look, chest tight with anxiety.

In the end Jesus did make it to Jairus's daughter and healed her as well. But every time I read that story, I'm struck by how fiercely present Jesus was, how he just would not let anything or anyone, even a medical emergency or a hurting father, rush him into the next moment.

And this story isn't a one-off, outlier, or enigma. Jesus was *constantly* interrupted—read the Gospels; half the stories are interruptions!—yet he never comes off as agitated or annoyed. (Well, he does with religious people—that's yet another book—but not at interruptions.)

Jesus' schedule was *full.* To the brim at times. In a good way. Yet he never came off *hurried.*

This rootedness in the moment and connectedness to God, other people, and himself weren't the by-products of a laid-back personality or pre–Wi-Fi world; they were the outgrowths of a way of life. A whole new way to be human that Jesus put on display in story after story.

After all, this is the man who waited three decades to preach his first sermon, and after one day on the job as Messiah, he went off to the wilderness for forty days to pray. Nothing could hurry this man.

Think with me about Jesus' lifestyle for a few minutes.

Jesus made sure to inject a healthy dose of margin into his life. It's been said that margin is "the space between our load and our limits."[4] For many of us there is *no* space between our loads and limits. We're not at 80 percent with room to breathe; we're at 100 *all the time.* Jesus' weekly schedule was a prophetic act against the hurried rhythms of our world.

He would regularly get up early and go off to a quiet place to be with his Father. There's a story where the disciples woke up and he was gone. Left before dawn, just to be alone and greet the day in the quiet.

Sometimes he would go away overnight or even for a few weeks at a time just to get away from the crowds and gather himself to God.

More than once we read stories about Jesus sleeping in and the disciples having to wake him up. I *like* this Jesus and want to follow him.

Every chance he got, he would enjoy a nice long meal with friends over a bottle of wine, creating space for in-depth conversations about the highs and lows of life.

He would practice Sabbath on a weekly basis—an entire day set aside for nothing but rest and worship, *every single week.*

Note his practice of simplicity, before it was cool, just the clothes on his back. You don't read any stories about him out shopping, hitting the mall for a new outfit for an appearance at the temple, or hunting online for a new pair of sandals when he already had fifteen back home. No, he lived "freely and lightly."[5] Free of all the discontent and distraction that comes from too much money and stuff we don't need.

We could go on, but my point is simple: he put on display an unhurried life, where space for God and love for people were the top priorities, and because he said *yes* to the Father and his kingdom, he constantly said *no* to countless other invitations.

Then he turned around and said, "Follow me."

Again: What does it mean to follow Jesus (or, as I prefer, apprentice under Jesus)? It's *very* simple. It means you live the way Jesus lived. You take his life and teachings as your template, your model, your pattern.

This means the central question of our apprenticeship to Jesus is pretty straightforward: *How would Jesus live if he were me?*

I mean, Jesus was a first-century, single Jewish rabbi, not a twenty-first-century parent, account manager, student, pastor, or professional *luchador,* so we have to ideate and transpose a bit.

Jesus wasn't a dad; I am. I imagine if he were dad to Jude, Moses, and Sunday, he would spend a lot of time with them. So I do that as an act of my apprenticeship to Jesus, who never had kids.

Say you're a new wife or mother. Jesus was neither, but your driving question is, How would he do this?

Or you're working on high-rise condo development. How would Jesus design this community?

You get the gist.

I think, for many of us, he would slow *way* down.

What we're really talking about here is a rule of life.

Stephen Covey (of *7 Habits* fame) said that we achieve inner peace when our schedule is aligned with our values. That line isn't from the Bible, but my guess is, if Jesus heard that, he would smile and nod.

Over the last few years, there's been an explosion of chatter in the self-help world over this idea of a fixed-hour schedule. Basically, you write up an ideal day or week or month on a blank calendar. You start with all your top priorities: the spiritual disciplines go in first if you're a follower of Jesus, then sleep, exercise, work, play, reading, margin, etc. And within reason you stick to it.

But most people don't realize this idea started not in the marketplace but in the monastery, not a decade ago but over a millennium ago, where monastic orders and often entire communities chose to do life together around a rule of life.

A rule was a schedule and set of practices to order your life around the way of Jesus in community. It was a way to keep from getting sucked into the hurry, busyness, noise, and distraction of regular life. A way to slow down. A way to live into what really matters: what Jesus called *abiding*.[6] Key relationships with family and community. The work God has set before us. A healthy soul. You know, the good stuff.

Don't let the language of a rule turn you off, especially if you're a high P on the Myers-Briggs and the idea sounds boring or legalistic. The word *rule* comes from the Latin word *regula,* which literally means "a straight piece of wood," (think: ruler), but it was also used for a trellis. Think of Jesus' teaching on abiding in the vine from John 15, one of his most important teachings on emotional health and spiritual life. Now think of a pleasant wine-tasting memory. What's underneath every thriving vine? A trellis. A structure to hold up the vine so it can grow and bear fruit.

You see the word picture?

What a trellis is to a vine, a rule of life is to abiding. It's a structure—in this case a schedule and a set of practices—to set up abiding as the central pursuit of your life. It's a way to organize all of your life around the practice of the presence of God, to work and rest and play and eat and drink and hang out with your friends and run errands and catch up on the news, *all* out of a place of deep, loving enjoyment of the Father's company.

If a vine doesn't have a trellis, it will die. And if your life with Jesus doesn't have some kind of structure to facilitate health and growth, it will wither away.

Following Jesus has to make it onto your schedule and into your practices or it will simply never happen. Apprenticeship to Jesus will remain an idea, not a reality in your life.

But here's the rub: most of us are too *busy* to follow Jesus.

Anytime I teach on a rule of life and some of the core practices for life with Jesus, I hear the same refrain:

"That sounds great, but I just don't have the time."

"I'm in grad school."

"I work a demanding job."

"I have little kids."

"I'm training for a marathon."

"I'm not an introvert like you."

Honestly, excuses. And I get it: I live in the same world. They are good excuses!

I used to smile and nod and let the awkward moment pass, but the older I get, the more I feel the courage to push back a little. Sometimes I'll graciously ask, "Are you really? How much time do you spend watching TV?" (This usually spawns a different kind of awkward moment.) "How much time do you spend online or on social media? Shopping?" I'll suggest people keep a time log for a week; when they do, they are usually *shocked* at how much time they give to trivial things.

Most of us have more than enough time to work with, even in busy seasons of life. We just have to reallocate our time to "seek first the kingdom of God,"[7] not the kingdom of entertainment.

And on the rare occasion (and it is *very* rare) that somebody genuinely does not have time for the practices we'll get into in part 3 of this book, I gently suggest that they are simply too busy, then, to follow Jesus.

No guilt trip. No shame. Again, not helpful. Just an honest appraisal.

The hard truth is that following Jesus is something you *do*. A *practice,* as much as a faith. At their core the practices of Jesus are about a relationship. With the God he called Father. And all relationships take time.

Let's say your marriage is less than ideal. Your spouse comes to you and asks for more time together, simply to enjoy each other and get back on the same page. He or she asks for, say, one date night a week, thirty minutes a day of conversation, and a little time on the weekends. Basically, the bare minimum for a healthy marriage.

If you say, "Sorry, I don't have the time" (all while giving thirty hours a week to things like TV and the internet and your fantasy football league), anybody with a modicum of common sense would say, "Yes, you do. You're just wasting your time." *Or,* he or she would say, "Well, then, you're just too busy to have a spouse. So either you need to radically rethink your schedule or you're en route to a divorce." Hopefully, you would advocate for the former.

Is our relationship with Jesus any different? We get out what we put in. This isn't some legalistic guilt trip. This is an *invitation.* To the life we actually ache for. A life that can be found only by moving through the world shoulder to shoulder with Jesus.

So I guess we come to a crossroads. A get-on-or-get-off moment. Are you ready to construct a trellis for your vine? A schedule, a practice (or two) to create space for life with Jesus? To make room for love and joy and peace to become your default settings?

Are you ready to arrange (or rearrange) your days so that Jesus' life becomes your new normal?

Intermission:

Wait, what are the spiritual disciplines again?

Before we move on to part 3, in which I lay out the four core practices that I find the most helpful in slowing down to experience health and life with Jesus, let me offer a brief summary of what the practices of Jesus (or what most call the spiritual disciplines) are.

Most of what we know about Jesus comes from the four Gospels. Essentially, the Gospels are biographies. Most of the content is stories, which is a bit strange, seeing as Jesus was a *teacher.* Matthew and John have the most teaching content per capita; Luke is in the middle; Mark has almost none. But the bulk of all four biographies is story, which makes sense, actually.

Think about biographies in general. Why do we read biographies? Usually, they're luminaries of some kind, and we read their life stories not just to know about them but also to become like them. (Or possibly to make sure we *don't* become like them.) To emulate their success or avoid their failure. In reading about *them*, we hope to better understand *ourselves;* in reading their stories, we hope to make sense of our own.

We tracking? Good. This is pretty straightforward.

And biographies are full of stories because if you want to emulate (or eschew) the life of Steve Jobs or Barack Obama or (insert your biography of choice), you don't just look at what he or she *said* or *did;* you look at *how* he or she *lived the details of day-to-day life.* If you're smart, you copy those details, make the individual's habits your habits; his or her routine, your routine; his or her values, your values in the hope that it will foster a similar kind of result in your own more ordinary life.

So, this person went to X law school, you go to X law school. He or she read an hour a day, you read an hour a day. He or she skipped breakfast? You throw out your bananas. The person was famous for an after-noon power nap? You buy a couch for your office. You copy all these details because you know the person you will even-tually become is the cumulative effect of thousands of tiny, seemingly mundane, or even insignificant details that in the end function like compound in-terest and create a life.

Still tracking? Good.

Here's the weird thing: *very few followers of Jesus read the four Gospels that way.*

We read them as cute sermon illustrations or allegorical pick-me-ups or theological gold mines. Again, not bad, but we often miss the proverbial forest for the trees. They are *biographies.*

I would argue that these stories about the details of Jesus' life have just as much to teach us about life in the kingdom as his teachings or miracles or the more major stories of his death and resurrection.

I mean that.

Now, Jesus' life rhythms, or the details of his lifestyle, have come to be called the "spiritual disciplines." That language isn't found in the New Testament, and there are pros and cons to that phrase. Unfortunately, most people think *spiritual* means "immaterial," but the spiritual disciplines are actually all habits of your mind and your body. I guess "mind-body disciplines" was trademarked or something? And discipline: I actually love that word, but in a hedonistic age it has negative connotations for most people, hence the decline of the spiritual disciplines in the Western church.[1]

I prefer to call them the "practices of Jesus." At the beginning and end of Jesus' Sermon on the Mount, he said this way of life is something you have to "put . . . into practice."[2]

If that language is still too religious sounding for you, just call them the habits of Jesus. That's nice, neutral language we're all familiar with.

Whatever you call them, these habits, practices, or spiritual disciplines are *how* we follow Jesus. How we adopt his lifestyle. How we create space for emotional health and spiritual life. Again, they are the trellis.

And like all habits, they are a means to an end. This is where well-meaning religious people (like myself) go wrong. When the spiritual disciplines (Bible reading, prayer, Sabbath, and so on) become an end in and of themselves, you've arrived at legalism. Therein lies death, not life.

The end is life to the full with Jesus. The end is to spend every waking moment in the conscious enjoyment of Jesus' company, to spend our entire lives with the most loving, joyful, peaceful person to ever live.

Back to the trellis metaphor: The point of a trellis isn't to make the vines stand up straight in neat rows, but rather to attain a rich, deep glass of wine. It's to create space for the vine to grow and bear fruit.

And unlike other types of habits, the practices of Jesus aren't just exercises for your mind and body to grow their willpower muscle and cultivate character. They are far more; *they are how we open our minds and bodies to a power far beyond our own and effect change.*

Think about it—what is a discipline? Not a spiritual discipline, just a discipline in general. Here's a pretty standard definition:

A discipline is any activity I can do by direct effort that

will eventually enable me
to do that which, currently,
I *cannot* do by direct effort.

For example, athletics (this is
the New Testament's most common example[3]). Let's say you
want to bench-press your own
weight but can't. (A scenario I
understand all too well.) You
don't have the power, the muscle,
to do that. It's not that you *can't*
do it; any healthy person can. It's
that you can't do it *yet.* You just
need access to more power. To
that end, you need to work out.
So a discipline is, say, a morning
push-up routine. That's something you *can* do. You start with
five. Then ten. You work your
way up to fifty. Eventually,

through discipline, you become the kind of person who can do something you previously could not do.

A discipline is a way to access power.

A *spiritual* discipline is similar but different. It's similar in that it's "any activity I can do by direct effort that will eventually enable me to do that which, currently, I *cannot* do by direct effort." It's a way to access power. But it's *different* in that not only are you exercising your own capacity to do the right thing (what we call *willpower*), but you are also opening yourself up to a power *far beyond your own*—that of the

Holy Spirit. You are creating time and space to access God himself at the deepest level of your being.

Here's Dallas Willard's definition of a spiritual discipline:

> The disciplines are activities of mind and body purposefully undertaken, to bring our personality and total being into effective cooperation with the divine order. They enable us more and more to live in a power that is, strictly speaking, beyond us, deriving from the spiritual realm itself.[4]

Willpower isn't bad; in fact, the recovery of our willpower is central to transformation. When willpower works, it works great. It just doesn't normally get you very far. Especially early on in your journey with Jesus. That's the rub.

But through practices—ordinary, easy, and, in my opinion, life-giving practices—grounded in the life of Jesus, we gain access to a life-power far beyond our own.

Ironically, the practices are almost never commanded by Jesus. The one exception is prayer, which is commanded multiple times. (Though you could argue prayer isn't a practice; it's the end goal of every practice if you define prayer as awareness of and connection to God.)

But Jesus never commands you to wake up in the morning and have a quiet time, read your Bible, live in community, practice Sabbath, give your money to the poor, or any of the core practices from his way.

He just *does these practices* and then says, "Follow me."

As we said earlier, many scholars argue a better translation of Jesus' original language is "Apprentice under me." Here's another option: "Copy the details of my life. Take the template of my day-to-day life as your own."

Jesus isn't anti-command, not by a long shot. But for Jesus, leadership isn't about coercion and control; it's about example and invitation.

He didn't command us to follow his practices; neither did he give lectures on how to do them or offer Saturday morning workshops on developing your own rule of life. He simply set the example of a whole new way to "carry life"; then he turned around and said, "If you're tired of the way you've been doing it and want rest for your souls, then come, take up the easy yoke, and copy the details of my life."

Okay, those are the practices. You still with me? Now we're ready to drill down on the easy yoke.

Part three:

Four practices for unhurrying your life

Silence and solitude

I'm just old enough to remember this thing from the late '90s
we called "boredom."

Anybody?

You digital natives have no clue what I'm talking about.
Boredom? Is that like when you have a bad Wi-Fi connection
and your Instagram feed takes more than two seconds to
load? Um, kind of. Just multiply that feeling by, well, *a lot.*

If you were born after, say, 1995, then you can't really remember a time when infinity wasn't in your front right pocket. But
I can.

There was a time when you'd be flying across the country,
somewhere over, say, Minnesota, and you'd finish your book

earlier than expected and just . . . stare out the window. With *nothing* to do.

Or you'd be waiting in line at your coffee shop of choice, five people ahead of you, and you'd have to just *stand* there. The extroverts in line would all strike up a conversation. We introverts would smile and nod, secretly thinking, *Why, dear God, is this total stranger talking to me?*

Anybody remember this? Waiting at the bus stop, stuck in traffic, sitting in the theater before a movie, in the back of a less-than-enthralling poli-sci class with nothing for your mind to do but wander through the infinite realm of possibility?

And while it's easy to sentimentalize something as inane as boredom, none of us, honestly, wants to go back to a pre-digital world. We're more efficient than ever. I get more done in less time than I ever dreamed possible a decade ago.

But again, pros and cons. We now have access to infinity through our new cyborgesque selves, which is great, but we've also lost something crucial. All those little moments of boredom were potential portals to prayer. Little moments throughout our days to wake up to the reality of God all around us. To wake up to our own souls. To draw our minds' attention (and, with it, devotion) back to God; to come off the hurry drug and come home to awareness.

Now all those little moments are gone, swallowed up by the digital carnivore. The second we feel even a hint of boredom coming on, we reach for the appendages that are our smart-phones: check our news feeds, answer an email (Reply All, click), read a tweet about Donald Trump's tweet about who-knows-what before we tweet about who-knows-what, look up the weather for Thursday, search for a new pair of shoes, and, naturally, slay at *Candy Crush.*

A survey from Microsoft found that 77 percent of young adults answered " 'yes' when asked, 'When nothing is occupying my attention, the first thing I do is reach for my phone.' "[1]

I mean, not *me.*

You.

Pretty much the only place we can be alone with our thoughts anymore is in the shower, and it's only a matter of time until our devices are waterproof, which, in turn, will trigger the apocalypse.

I allow myself that brief rant just to say that all this has profound implications for our apprenticeships to Jesus and our experiences (or *lack* of experiences) of the life he has on offer. How so? Simple: this new normal of hurried digital distraction is robbing us of the ability to be *present.*

Present to God.

Present to other people.

Present to all that is good, beautiful, and true in our world.

Even present to our own souls.

Once again, Andrew Sullivan, in his manifesto for silence in an age of noise, wrote this:

> There are books to be read; landscapes to be walked;
> friends to be with; life to be fully lived. . . . This new
> epidemic of distraction is our civilization's specific weak-
> ness. And its threat is not so much to our minds, even as
> they shape-shift under the pressure. The threat is to our
> souls. At this rate, if the noise does not relent, we might
> even forget we have any.[2]

The noise of the modern world makes us deaf to the voice of God, drowning out the one input we most need.

I mean, how do we have any kind of spiritual life at all if we can't pay attention longer than a goldfish? How do you pray, read the Scriptures, sit under a teaching at church, or rest well on the Sabbath when every chance you get, you reach for the dopamine dispenser that is your phone?

To requote the Catholic father and social critic Ronald Rolheiser, "We . . . are distracting ourselves into spiritual oblivion."[3]

So, rant over.

Now, a question: Is there a practice from the way of Jesus that could help with this? A time-tested art form—or, if you prefer, spiritual discipline—that could set us up to thrive *right in the middle* of the chaos of modern society?

Answer: Yes. Absolutely. Actually, there are quite a few. We'll talk about my top four for unhurrying your life. Let's start with what I think are the most important of them all: silence and solitude.

Jesus and the quiet place

From the beginning, then.

At the end of Matthew 3, there's a fascinating story about Jesus' baptism. When he came up out of the water, there was literally a voice from heaven saying, "This is my Son, whom I love; with him I am well pleased."[4] This is more than an emotional high. Or even a spiritual high. This is *the* launch-pad from which Jesus is sent out into the world.

But in the very next line, we read this:

> Then Jesus was led by the Spirit into the desert to be tempted by the devil. After fasting forty days and forty nights, he was hungry. The tempter came to him.[5]

Notice, the first thing Jesus did after his baptism was head straight into the desert.

Desert here doesn't necessarily mean sand and heat. The Greek word is *eremos,* and it has a wide array of meanings. It can be translated

- desert
- deserted place
- desolate place

- solitary place

- lonely place

- quiet place (my personal favorite)

- wilderness

There are stories—lots of them—in all four Gospels about Jesus' relationship to the eremos, but this is the first story. And I want you to see it because it's the starting place for his ministry and mission. But it's an odd story, right? Have you ever read that line—"Jesus was led by the Spirit into the desert to be tempted by the devil"—and thought to yourself, *What's up with* that?

I mean, if you've been reading the Bible from *Genesis* up to *Matthew,* you get that Jesus has to go toe-to-toe with the devil. The protagonist must face the bad-guy-to-end-all-bad-guys. Evil has to be defeated. You get that.

But why in the wilderness? Why alone? And why after forty days of fasting? When he's hungry?

For years this story made no sense to me because I thought of the wilderness as the place of *weakness.*

I read it this way: Isn't that so like the devil? To come at us at the end of a long day or a long week? When we're hangry and at our worst?

But then I realized I had it backward.

The wilderness isn't the place of weakness; it's the place of *strength.*

"Jesus was led by the Spirit into the wilderness" because it was there, and only there, that Jesus was at the height of his spiritual powers. It was only after a month and a half of prayer and fasting in the quiet place that he had the capacity to take on the devil himself and walk away unscathed.

That's why, over and over again, you see Jesus come back to the eremos.

Take Mark 1 as an example. Mark 1 is essentially one long chapter about Jesus' first day on the job as the Messiah. It was a marathon day; he was up early, teaching in the synagogue, then healing Peter's mother-in-law over lunch, then up late healing the sick and demonized. He must have been well beyond exhausted.

Yet then we read this:

> Very early in the morning, while it was still dark, Jesus got up, left the house and went off to a solitary place [eremos], where he prayed.[6]

You would think Jesus would have slept in, gone for a light run, and then had brunch with his disciples. Nothing says post-Sunday recovery like a farmer's scramble.

But instead Jesus was up early and out the door to the quiet place.

To clarify, Jesus went to the quiet place for a month and a half. Came back to Capernaum for *one day* of busy activity. Then he headed straight back to the eremos to pray.

Meaning, the quiet place wasn't a onetime thing. It was an ongoing part of his life rhythm.

But the story isn't over:

> Simon and his companions went to look for him, and when they found him, they exclaimed: "Everyone is looking for you!"[7]

Here's my paraphrase:

> Jesus, where have you *been*? You were amazing yesterday. Word's out. *Vogue* is calling for an interview. TMZ is hiding outside Peter's house. #Jesus is trending. We need you back, *post-haste.*[8]

And what did Jesus say?

> Let us go somewhere else—to the nearby villages—so I can preach there also. That is why I have come.[9]

That's Jesus for *no.*

Notice, Jesus came out of the wilderness with all sorts of clarity about his identity and calling. He was grounded. Centered. In touch with God *and* himself. From that place of emotional equilibrium and spiritual succor, he knew precisely what to say yes to and, just as importantly, what to say no to.

Hence: as the Gospels go on, you quickly realize the quiet place was top priority for Jesus.

There's a story in Mark 6 where the disciples were just dead tired after a few weeks of kingdom work. We read:

> So many people were coming and going that they did not even have a chance to eat.[10]

Ever feel like that? All you parents are thinking, *Every single day.*

And to his overbusy, overtired apprentices, Jesus said:

> Come with me by yourselves to a quiet place [eremos] and get some rest.[11]

Translation:

> What you really need isn't a beer or a night out at the movies. What you really need is time alone with me. But to do that, we need to get away from all the noise and people.

So,

> They went away by themselves in a boat to a solitary place [eremos].[12]

Sounds nice. Time alone with Jesus at a spa by the Sea of Galilee. Organic tea, anybody? Unfortunately, that's not how the story goes.

Next lines:

> But many who saw them leaving recognized them and
> ran on foot from all the towns and got there ahead of
> them. When Jesus landed and saw a large crowd, he had
> compassion on them, because they were like sheep
> without a shepherd. So he began teaching them many
> things.
>   By this time it was late in the day.[13]

I love the realism of this story. There are times when what you
really need is time alone with Jesus, but, well, life happens.
People happen. You set aside time to Sabbath or pray or just
take a night off with no plan, but then you get a text from your
boss, a minor crisis at work. Your two-year-old swallows a
Lego Kylo Ren. You google "Closest emergency room." Your
roommate had a bad day and could use a chat. Two hours
later she's still crying. Thousands of people are banging down
your front door asking for you to heal them and teach about
the kingdom of God because they believe you're the long-
awaited Messiah. Y'know, ordinary life stuff.

Sound familiar? You ever feel like, try as you might, you just
can't get time to rest? You're in good company with Jesus
himself.

But again, that's still not the end of the story. A boy's back-
pack and five thousand lunches later, we read this:

> Jesus made his disciples get into the boat and go on
> ahead of him to Bethsaida, while he dismissed the crowd.
> After leaving them, he went up on a mountainside to pray.

Later that night, . . . he was alone on land.[14]

I used to read the ending to this story and think, *Wow, Jesus is so spiritual—up all night praying!* And he was. But notice *why* he was up all night praying. Because it was the only time he could find to be alone in the quiet! He was so busy that he literally didn't have a moment alone all day long, so all he could think to do was send his apprentices away and stay up all night on a mountain (the word *eremos* isn't used here, but a mountaintop at midnight fits the bill). Because he knew that time alone with his Father was even more important than sleep itself.

And we haven't even gotten to Luke's gospel yet.

In Luke, Jesus went to his quiet place no less than *nine* times. Just one more story; then I'll stop. I promise. This one is from Luke 5:

> The news about [Jesus] spread all the more, so that crowds of people came to hear him and to be healed of their sicknesses.

Crowds banging down Jesus' front door was a regular thing. But look at the next line:

> Jesus often withdrew to lonely places and prayed.[15]

In Greek that phrase "lonely places" is . . . Well, I'm guessing you know what it is by now.

I love this. Jesus "often withdrew." He frequently got away. He made a point to sneak off to pray on a regular basis. It was a common habit in his repertoire.

In Luke's gospel in particular, you can chart Jesus' life along two axis points: the busier and more in demand and famous Jesus became, and the *more* he withdrew to his quiet place to pray.

Usually for us it's the exact opposite. When we get overbusy and life is hectic and people are vying for our time, the quiet place is the first thing to go *rather than our first go to.* The first thing we lose is unhurried time to just sit with God in the quiet. To pray. Read a psalm. Take an internal inventory. Let our souls catch up to our bodies.

In seasons of busyness we need *more* time in the quiet place, not less, definitely not less. And if you're running through your Rolodex of excuses right now—I'm a full-time mom, I have a demanding job that starts early, I'm an extrovert, I have ADHD, etc.—stop for a minute. Think about this: *Jesus* needed time in the quiet place.

I repeat, *Jesus* needed time.

And a fair bit of it.

You think you don't?

Silence and solitude

Through the years this practice of Jesus has come to be called "silence and solitude."

As simple as that sounds, there's a lot to it.

So, a word on each.

First, silence.

There are two dimensions of silence—*external* and *internal.*

External silence is pretty self-explanatory: no noise. No music in your headphones. No TV, even in the background. No roommate playing *Fortnite* down the hall. No toddler scream-ing, *Packie! Packie! Packie!* No chatting to your mom over the phone while emptying the dishwasher. It's when you're up early or out in nature or in your room, and it's *quiet.* When your ears are humming with the din of silence.

Quiet is a spiritual discipline in and of itself. A millennium and a half ago, the African theologian Saint Augustine said entering silence is "entering into joy."[16]

I'm writing this particular chapter from Melbourne, Australia. I spent the last few days teaching on a jam-packed schedule, and it was great, really fun, but *loud*—nonstop noise, people, activity, stimuli. Naturally, I woke up this morning extremely tired. But compliments of jet lag, I also woke up early and had plenty of time to get a run in before church. I ran along the Yarra River in Fitzroy Gardens, which is reminiscent of another garden, Eden. There was nobody in the park. Just me, the river, a light breeze playing with the eucalyptus trees over my head . . . and God. About twenty minutes into my run, I felt my soul wake back up. God's presence wasn't an idea in my head but a felt experience. All around me, *in* me.

And I wasn't even praying, really, much less reading my Bible or doing anything spiritual in intent. It was just something about the quiet. Quiet is a kind of balm for emotional healing. And more: an unlocked, open door to spiritual life. As Saint John Climacus, the sixth-century Syrian monk who spent most of his life praying on Mount Sinai, so beautifully said, "The friend of silence draws near to God."[17]

Nobody ever said the same about noise. In fact, C. S. Lewis, in his masterwork of satire, *The Screwtape Letters,* has the demons railing against silence as a danger to their cause (the ruin of a Christian's soul). Senior demon Screwtape calls the devil's realm a "Kingdom of Noise" and claims, "We will make the whole universe a noise in the end."[18]

Could that be why we let so much noise run roughshod over our lives?

Or is it something else?

Where does this strange urge come from to reach for NPR the moment we get in our cars? Or always have music on in the background? Or flip on the TV while we're cooking dinner? Or listen to podcasts during our workouts?

As easy as it is to blame the devil, could it be that we're using external noise to drown out *internal* noise?

Here's what I mean by internal noise: the mental chatter that just never shuts up. The running commentary in our heads on *everything.* The replaying of a lousy conversation with a friend over and over again. Our lustful thoughts for the girl or guy down the street. Our fantasies. And not just sexual; our revenge fantasies—imagining saying *this* or doing *that* to our enemies of choice. Our worry—the chipping away at our joy and peace with the hammer of "what if?" The obsessing over hypothetical scenarios, role-playing the future, catastrophizing. Idealizing. Dreaming of the perfect life, which in turn poisons our actual lives.

The clutter in our minds is like a mental hoarder, landlocked in his or her bedroom in a self-constructed prison. Some of us feel trapped in the toxic, unhealthy patterns of our own minds.

External noise is easy to quiet. Just turn off your phone. Power down the stereo. Lie on your couch. Or walk to the park. Or book a night at a cabin close by. Or maybe even a monastery. Easy.

But internal noise? That's a whole other animal. A wild beast in desperate need of taming. There's no off switch.

The kind of silence I'm talking about is when you silence *both.*

So, that's silence.

Then, solitude.

Again, solitude is pretty straightforward. It's when you're alone, with God and with your own soul.

For clarification, by *solitude* I don't mean isolation. The two are worlds apart.

Solitude is engagement; isolation is escape.

Solitude is safety; isolation is danger.

Solitude is how you open yourself up to God; isolation is painting a target on your back for the tempter.

Solitude is when you set aside time to feed and water and nourish your soul. To let it grow into health and maturity. Isolation is what you crave when you neglect the former.

And solitude—as somber as it sounds—is anything but loneliness. In his masterpiece *Celebration of Discipline,* Richard Foster wrote, "Loneliness is inner emptiness. Solitude is inner fulfillment."[19] In solitude we're anything but alone. In fact, that's where many of us feel *most* in connection to God.

As we said earlier, one of the great problems of spirituality in our day and age that so few people feel safe enough to admit is how separated we feel from God. We rarely experience God's presence throughout our day. "Love, joy, and peace" does not describe the felt experience of many Christians. Often we come to church hoping for a God hit—a fleeting moment of connection to God before we return to the secular wasteland.

Could the antidote for this spiritual malaise be as "easy" as silence and solitude?

If our theory is right and the problem is more *our* absence than *his,* more about our distraction than his disconnection,[20] then the solution is fairly simple: create an environment for attention and connection to God; and I know of no better place than the eremos.

Why this is of life-and-death importance

Through church history most of the master teachers of the way of Jesus have agreed: silence and solitude are the most important of all the spiritual disciplines.

Henri Nouwen said it bluntly, yet eloquently:

> Without solitude it is virtually impossible to live a spiritual life. . . .
> We do not take the spiritual life seriously if we do not set aside some time to be with God and listen to him.[21]

Notice the lack of nuance. No exceptions to the rule. No self-deprecating story to soften the blow. He's just honest: if you don't set aside time to be alone with God, your relationship will wither on the vine.

Again, this makes sense. Your relationship to God is no different than any other relationship—it takes time alone together. What would happen to my marriage if Tammy and I were never alone together? Never had time to talk in private, share our deepest, darkest secrets, our dreams, our fears? Make love? Just *be,* shoulder to shoulder, alone together? Obviously our marriage would suffer, if not die eventually. The same is true of your relationship to God. And even to your own soul.

There's a saying in parenting literature: "To a child, love is spelled T-I-M-E." There's truth in that. And not just for parents and children. If you love God the Father and want a living, thriving relationship with him where you experience his presence all through the day, then you need to carve out time to be alone with him. Full stop. And relational time is wildly inefficient. It comes in fits and bursts. You spend a day together, but it's one short conversation you remember, a passing comment that changes everything.

Nouwen once asked Mother Teresa for spiritual direction; he was dealing with a number of problems in his soul and sought her wisdom. Imagine one of the greatest followers of Jesus of the twentieth century asking a saint for a little advice on how to follow Jesus. Oh to be a fly on that wall.

You know what she said?

> Well, when you spend one hour a day adoring your Lord and never do anything which you know is wrong . . . you will be fine![22]

So, so simple. Two very straightforward practices. Just take an hour a day to enjoy God. Oh, and don't do anything you know is wrong.

So before you write me off and go back to your noisy life—and, I might add, before you write off Mother Teresa, Henri Nouwen, and *Jesus,* who hopefully carry more weight than yours truly—just think about what's at stake.

When we *don't* practice this Jesus soul habit, we reap the

consequences:

- We feel distant from God and end up living off somebody else's spirituality, via a podcast feed or book or one-page devotional we read before we rush out the door to work.

- We feel distant from *ourselves.* We lose sight of our identities and callings. We get sucked into the tyranny of the urgent, not the important.

- We feel an undercurrent of anxiety that rarely, if ever, goes away. This sense that we're *always* behind, always playing catch up, never done.

- Then we get exhausted. We wake up, and our first thoughts are, *Already? I can't wait to go to bed . . .* We lag through our days, our low-grade energy on loan from our stimulants of choice. Even when we catch up on our sleep, we feel a deeper kind of tired.

- Then we turn to our escapes of choice. We run out of energy to do what's actually life giving for our souls, say, prayer. And instead we turn to the cheap fix—another glass of wine, a new show streaming online, our social media feeds, porn.

- We become easy prey for the tempter. Just furthering our sense of distance from God and our souls.

- Then emotional unhealth sets in. We start living from the surface of our lives, not the core. We're reactionary. The smallest thing is a trigger—a throwaway line from the boss, a snide comment from a coworker, a suggestion from a spouse or roommate—it doesn't take much. We lose our tempers. Bark at our kids. Get defensive. Sulk. Feel angry or sad, often both.

These are the signs and symptoms of a life without silence and solitude. On the flip side, here's the alternative:

- We find our quiet places—a park down the street, a reading nook at home, a morning routine that begins before the little ones are awake—and we "come away."[23]

- We take our time. Maybe it's not a full hour, but we're there long enough to decompress from all the noise and traffic and stress and nonstop stimulation of modern society. Sometimes all we need is a few minutes. Other times, an hour isn't enough. Other times, we gratefully take what time we can get.

- We slow down. Breathe. Come back to the *present*.

- We start to feel. At first we feel the whole gamut of human emotions—not just joy and gratitude and celebration and restfulness but also sadness and doubt and anger and anxiety. Usually I feel all the lousy emotions first. That's just how it goes.

- We face the good, the bad, and the ugly in our own hearts. Our worry. Our depression. Our hope. Our desire for God; *our lack of desire for God.* Our sense of God's presence; *our sense of his absence.* Our fantasies; our realities. All the lies we believe; the truth we come home to. Our

motivations. Our addictions. The coping mecha-
nisms we reach for just to make it through the
week. All this is exposed and painfully so. But
rather than leaking out on those we love most, it's
exposed in the safe place of the Father's love and
voice.

- In our ears we sense his voice cut through the
cacophony of all the other voices, which slowly
fade to the deafening roar of silence. In that
silence we hear God speak his love over us.
Speak our identities and callings into being. We
get his perspective on life and our humble, good
places in it.

And we come to a place of freedom. Our failures slowly lose
their power over us. As do our successes. We get out from
under the tyranny of other people's opinions—their disap-
proval or approval of us. Free to just be *us,* the mixed bag we
are. Nothing more than children with our Father. Adopted into
love. Free to be in process yet to arrive, and that's okay. In
silence and solitude our souls finally come home. That's what
Jesus meant by "abide,"[24] the verb of *abode* or *home.* The
place of rest. We come back to our places of soul rest. To
what Thomas Kelly called "the unhurried [center of] peace
and power."[25]

As I see it, we have two options.

Option A: we neglect this practice, make excuses, get sucked
into the rat race, and face emotional unhealth *at best* and
"spiritual oblivion" at worst.

Or B: we recapture this ancient yet timely practice and experience the life of Jesus.

The whole world is talking about this right now. You can't go three feet in a bookstore or peruse TED.com without hearing all the buzz around *mindfulness.* And mindfulness is simply silence and solitude for a secular society. It's the same thing, just missing the best part—Jesus. The way the story is usually told, mindfulness is a derivative of Buddhism, updated by secular psychotherapeutic technique. But there's a solid case that it's more Jesus than Buddha. More Sermon on the Mount than *Siddhartha.* More Saint Teresa of Ávila than Thich Nhat Hanh. But of course, our post-Christian culture is a reaction *against* Christianity, so Buddhism is in (which works well since it's essentially a religion without God) and Jesus is out. Okay, sure. But followers of Jesus have been doing this for thousands of years; we just called it *prayer* or *meditation* or *contemplation.* We have two millennia of tradition and wisdom and best practices to draw from.

Again, Andrew Sullivan wrote this:

> Modernity slowly weakened spirituality, by design and accident, in favor of commerce; it downplayed silence and mere being in favor of noise and constant action. The reason we live in a culture increasingly without faith is not because science has somehow disproved the unprovable, but because the white noise of secularism has removed the very stillness in which it might endure or be reborn. . . .
> If the churches came to understand that the greatest threat to faith today is not hedonism but distraction,

perhaps they might begin to appeal anew to a frazzled digital generation.[26]

My fellow denizens of a "frazzled digital generation," let's go with option B.

Of course this is easier said than done. Most people find this practice extremely hard to do, and not just extroverts. Many would say it's the most difficult and most radical of *all* the practices. (Cue what I said earlier about all the emotions you've been running away from sneaking up on you . . .)

And yet: it's so easy that you just take a little time each day to be alone in the quiet with yourself and God. Ideally, you add in some longer stints, say, on the Sabbath (next chapter, keep reading) or a periodic retreat. But it's more resting than working, more about *not* doing than doing, subtraction not addition. It's "easy," and (as is true of all the practices) it makes the rest of life even *easier.*

I grew up in a church tradition where we started our days with a quiet time. At the very beginning of our days, we would set aside a chunk of time to do Jesusy stuff. Usually there was coffee involved. Normally we read the Bible. Asked God to do some things in our lives. Confessed our screwups, our needs, our aches. Sometimes we just sat there. Alone. In the quiet. With God. And our souls.

Why doesn't anybody talk about that anymore? Or, when they do, why do people mock it or shrug it off as some legalistic hangover from fundamentalism?

I have a secret. Don't judge me. I still practice a quiet time.

Every day.

I wouldn't miss it for the world. It's usually the *best* part of my day, hands down. And I'm not even a morning person.

I say we bring back the quiet time. Rock it like it's 1999.

Here's to tomorrow morning, six o'clock. Coffee. The chair by the window, the window by the tree. Time to breathe. A psalm and story from the Gospels. Hearing the Father's voice. Pouring out my own. Or just sitting, resting. Maybe I'll hear a word from God that will alter my destiny; maybe I'll just process my anger over something that's bothering me. Maybe I'll feel my mind settle like untouched water; maybe my mind will ricochet from thought to thought, and never come to rest. If so, that's fine. I'll be back, same time tomorrow. Starting my day in the quiet place.

You?

Sabbath

I got out of bed this morning because I *wanted* something. Quite a few things, actually.

I wanted to watch the sunrise over a cup of coffee . . .

I wanted to spend time alone with God before the three-headed chaos monster (that is, Jude, Moses, and Sunday) was out of its lair and needed to feed . . .

I wanted to make my writing deadline for this book, to make a living, to put food on the table for my family . . .

My point is, I woke up with all sorts of desires, and those desires are what got me out of bed on a cold and dark winter's day.

Desire is a great motivator. It's the engine of our lives; its function is to propel us out of bed and out into the world.

But.

If at any point desire is no longer under our control and is instead driving our lives, we're in trouble. Because when you take a closer look at the dynamics of desire, you realize desire is one of those things that is never, *ever* satisfied.

As far back as 1000 BC, the Qoheleth of Ecclesiastes said:

> The eye is not satisfied with seeing.[1]

A more recent poet simply said:

> I can't get no satisfaction.[2]

Same idea.

That towering intellect of the thirteenth century, Thomas Aquinas, once asked the question, What would satisfy our desire? What would it take to *feel* satisfied? The answer he came up with was this: everything. We would have to experience everything and everybody and *be* experienced *by* everything and everybody to feel satisfied. Eat at every restaurant; travel to every country, every city, every exotic locale; experience every natural wonder; make love to every partner we could possibly desire; win every award; climb to the top of every field; own every item in the world; etc. We would have to experience it *all* to ever feel . . . okay, that's enough. Sadly, even if we had access to unlimited funds, time and space still have a pesky way of getting in the way.

Karl Rahner, who was one of the most important Catholic theologians of the twentieth century, had this haunting line:

> In the torment of the insufficiency of everything attainable, we learn that ultimately in this world there is no finished symphony.[3]

I love his word picture of an unfinished symphony. For those of us a little more lowbrow, think of a Chance The Rapper song cut off right before the end. Can you imagine it? The *argh* . . . . . . ? The frustrated sense of incompletion? Of a melody unresolved? Not at rest?

That feeling *is* the human condition.

What these poets and prophets and preachers are all tapping into is the reality that *desire is infinite.* It has no limit. No point at which it's ever satisfied. The problem is, *we are finite;* we have all sorts of limits, remember? So the result is restlessness.

Or in the language of math: infinite desire – finite soul = restlessness.

We live with chronically unsatisfied desires. Like an itch that no matter how many times you scratch doesn't go away. No matter how much we see, do, buy, sell, eat, drink, experience, visit, etc., we always want more.

The question for us as apprentices of Jesus, or really as humans, is simple: What do we do with all this pent-up, unsatisfied desire? This restlessness?

The Jesus tradition would offer this: human desire is infinite because we were made to live with God forever in his world and nothing less will ever satisfy us, so our only hope is to put desire back in its proper place on God. And to put all our other desires in their proper place *below* God. Not to detach from all desire (as in Stoicism or Buddhism), but to come to the place where we no longer need _____ to live a happy, restful life.

One of the most famous lines of the way of Jesus post–New Testament is from Saint Augustine. Writing at the fall of the Roman Empire, the bishop of Hippo said this:

> You have made us for yourself, and our heart is restless until it rests in you.[4]

More recently, Dallas Willard put it this way:

> Desire is infinite partly because we were made by God, made for God, made to need God, and made to run on God. We can be satisfied only by the one who is infinite, eternal, and able to supply all our needs; we are only at home in God. When we fall away from God, the desire for the infinite remains, but it is displaced upon things that will certainly lead to destruction.[5]

Ultimately, nothing in this life, apart from God, can satisfy our desires. Tragically, we continue to chase after our desires ad infinitum. The result? A chronic state of restlessness or, worse, angst, anger, anxiety, disillusionment, depression—all of which lead to a life of *hurry,* a life of busyness, overload, shopping, materialism, careerism, a life of more . . . which in turn makes us even *more* restless. And the cycle spirals out of control.

To make a bad problem worse, this is exacerbated by our cultural moment of digital marketing from a society built around the twin gods of accumulation and accomplishment.

Advertising is literally an attempt to monetize our restlessness. They say we see upward of four *thousand* ads a day, all designed to stoke the fire of desire in our bellies. Buy this. Do this. Eat this. Drink this. Have this. Watch this. Be this. In his book on the Sabbath, Wayne Muller opined, "It is as if we have inadvertently stumbled into some horrific wonderland."[6]

Social media takes this problem to a whole new level as we live under the barrage of images—not just from marketing departments but from the rich and famous as well as our friends and family, all of whom curate the best moments of their lives. This ends up unintentionally playing to a core sin of the human condition that goes all the way back to the garden—envy. The greed for another person's life and the loss of gratitude, joy, and contentment in our own.

And when our innate human restlessness collides with the digital age, the result is a culture-wide crisis of emotional unhealth and spiritual death.

So . . .

Is there a practice from the life and teachings of Jesus to mitigate against the chronic restlessness of our condition and culture and to tap into Jesus' rest for our souls? You already know the answer: *heck* yes. Many, but at the top of the list is Sabbath.

The Sabbath

The word *Sabbath* comes to us from the Hebrew *Shabbat.* The word literally means "to stop." The Sabbath is simply a day to stop: stop working, stop wanting, stop worrying, just *stop.*

Think of the images that come to us through lifestyle advertising—in our social media feeds or that trendy magazine on the coffee table. The couple lounging in a king-size bed over breakfast and coffee, organic linen spilling onto the floor; the photo-perfect picnic at the beach with wine, cheese, and that trendy bathing suit; a twentysomething playing guitar on the couch while watching the rain fall. Whether they are selling a new bathrobe, a down comforter, or a piece of furniture, almost all of them are images of Sabbath. Of stopping.

The marketing wing of Blue Dot or *Kinfolk* and *Cereal* magazines know that you ache for this kind of a stopping-rich life, *but you don't have it.* And they are tapping into your restlessness, hoping to cash in. The irony is, to get this feeling, you don't need to pay $99.99 for a terry cloth bathrobe or $69.99 for a handmade throw blanket. You just need to Sabbath, to stop. You just need to take a day of your week to slow down, breathe.

But Sabbath is more than just a day; it's a *way of being* in the world. It's a spirit of restfulness that comes from abiding, from living in the Father's loving presence all week long.

You could frame it like this:

Restfulness	Relentlessness
Margin	Busyness
Slowness	Hurry
Quiet	Noise
Deep relationships	Isolation
Time alone	Crowds
Delight	Distraction
Enjoyment	Envy
Clarity	Confusion
Gratitude	Greed
Contentment	Discontentment
Trust	Worry
Love	Anger, angst
Joy	Melancholy, sadness
Peace	Anxiety
Working from love	Working for love
Work as contribution	Work as accumulation and accomplishment

Which list best describes you? If you resonate more with list B, again, zero guilt trip. Human nature and the digital age form a foreboding alliance *against* a spirit of restfulness. We all struggle in this area.

No wonder the writer of Hebrews, speaking of Sabbath and its spirit of restfulness, called us to "make every effort to enter that rest."[7] Notice the irony of that command; we are to work hard to rest well.

There is a discipline to the Sabbath that is really hard for a lot of us. It takes a lot of intentionality: it won't just happen to you. It takes planning and preparation. It takes self-control, the capacity to say no to a list of good things so you can say yes to the best. But Sabbath is the primary discipline, or practice, by which we cultivate the spirit of restfulness in our lives *as a whole.* The Sabbath is to a spirit of restfulness what a soccer practice is to a match or band practice is to a show. It's how we practice, how we prepare our minds and bodies for the moments that matter most.

Walter Brueggemann has this great line: "People who keep sabbath live all seven days differently."[8] It's true. Watch out for the Sabbath. It will mess with you. First it will mess with one day of your week; then it will mess with your whole life.

To clarify, Sabbath isn't *less* than a day; it's a whole lot more. Hence, it was woven into the fabric of Jesus' weekly routine.

Jesus on the Sabbath

It was a lazy Saturday afternoon: hot with clear skies overhead. Jesus was hiking through a cornfield with his apprentices, like you do. It was the Sabbath, and this is one of many stories about Jesus and the seventh day. Built into Jesus' life rhythm was a core practice—an *entire* day, every week, set aside just to slow down, to stop.

But on this particular Sabbath, Jesus got in trouble with the Pharisees. They took issue with how Jesus and his friends were celebrating the day, royally missing the heart of God behind this practice. In a loving rebuke Jesus simply said:

> The Sabbath was made for man, not man for the Sabbath.[9]

What a stunning line. Here we are, thousands of years later, reading and rereading it. Yet sadly, often *misreading* it. In context, Jesus was beating up on a legalistic, guilt-heavy religious culture that had totally missed the Father's heart behind the command to slow down one day a week. Translation: a culture that was (in this area) the *exact opposite* of our own.

First-century Jews needed to hear the second half of that command: "The Sabbath was made for man, *not man for the Sabbath.*" They had it backward, cart before the horse and all that.

Fast-forward to the twenty-first century: we aren't legalistic about the Sabbath—most of us don't even practice Sabbath *at all.* A day off? Sure. Sunday worship? When I can. But *Sabbath*? Very few of us even know what that is, exactly.

The Sabbath isn't a new idea; it predates Jesus by millennia. It's just new *to us.*[10]

My fellow Portlander and dear friend A. J. Swoboda wrote this:

[The Sabbath] has largely been forgotten by the church, which has uncritically mimicked the rhythms of the industrial and success-obsessed West. The result? Our road-weary, exhausted churches have largely failed to integrate Sabbath into their lives as vital elements of Christian discipleship. It is not as though we do not love God—we love God deeply. We just do not know how to sit with God anymore.

He continued:

We have become perhaps the most emotionally exhausted, psychologically overworked, spiritually malnourished people in history.[11]

I would argue that twenty-first-century Americans (and, yes, to all my friends in the UK and Australia and Iceland, you too . . .) need to hear the *first* half of that command: "The Sabbath was made for man." It was created, designed, by God himself. And it's "for" us. A gift to enjoy from the Creator to the creation. To gratefully receive.

In his iconic one-line teaching on the Sabbath, Jesus was tapping into a practice as old as the earth itself. A practice that goes all the way back to Genesis 1.

In the beginning . . .

So the story of the Bible starts with, "In the beginning God created the heavens and the earth." But after six days of hard work to get the universe up and running, we read the following:[12]

By the seventh day God had finished the work he had been doing; so on the seventh day he rested from all his work. Then God blessed the seventh day and made it holy, because on it he rested from all the work of creating that he had done.[13]

Did you catch that?

God rested.

"Yeah, I'm not really into the Sabbath. I'm an extrovert and I just like to stay busy and . . ."

God rested.

"Yeah, I get the Sabbath thing, but I work a demanding job that I love, and I just can't make the time because . . ."

God rested.

"Yeah, but I have two little kids at home, and it's just not really doable right now. Maybe later when . . ."

Do I need to say it again?

God rested.

And in doing so, he built a rhythm into the DNA of creation. A tempo, a syncopated beat. God worked for six, rested for one.

When we fight this work-six-days, Sabbath-one-day rhythm, we go against the grain of the universe. And to quote the philosopher H. H. Farmer, "If you go against the grain of the universe, you get splinters."[14]

I've had people laugh off the call to Sabbath with a terrible cliché: "Yeah, well, the devil never takes a day off."

Ummm, last time I checked, the devil loses. Plus, he's the *devil.*

The last time a society tried to abandon the seven-day week was during the revolution in France. They switched to a ten-day workweek to up productivity. The rise of the proletariat! And? Disaster—the economy crashed, the suicide rate skyrocketed, and productivity? It went *down.* It's been proven by study after study: there is zero correlation between hurry and productivity. In fact, once you work a certain number of hours in a week, your productivity plummets. Wanna know what the number is? Fifty hours. Ironic: that's about a six-day workweek. One study found that there was zero difference in productivity between workers who logged seventy hours and those who logged fifty-five.[15] Could God be speaking to us even through our bodies?

My point: This rhythm isn't the by-product of human ingenuity—the ancient version of *The 7 Habits of Highly Effective People*—that we're free to adapt or change as we see fit for the modern era. It's the way a brilliant mind designed our souls and society to flourish and thrive.

Fight it, fight God.

Fight God, fight our own souls.

Now, what does the writer of *Genesis* mean by "rested"? Was God tired? Burned out?

As I've said, the Hebrew word *Shabbat* means "to stop." But it can also be translated "to delight." It has this dual idea of stopping and also of joying in God and our lives in his world. The Sabbath is an entire day set aside to follow God's example, to stop and delight.

To delight in the world . . .

In our lives in it . . .

And above all, in God himself.

If you're new to the Sabbath, a question to give shape to your practice is this: What could I do for twenty-four hours that would fill my soul with a deep, throbbing joy? That would make me spontaneously combust with wonder, awe, gratitude, and praise?

Dan Allender, in his book *Sabbath,* had this to say:

> The Sabbath is an invitation to enter delight. The Sabbath, when experienced as God intended, is the best day of our lives. Without question or thought, it is the best day of the week. It is the day we anticipate on Wednesday, Thursday, and Friday—and the day we remember on Sunday, Monday, and Tuesday. Sabbath is the holy time where we feast, play, dance, have sex, sing, pray, laugh, tell stories, read, paint, walk, and watch creation in its fullness. Few people are willing to enter the Sabbath and

sanctify it, to make it holy, because a full day of delight and joy is more than most people can bear in a lifetime, let alone a week.[16]

And all this is rooted in God. He rested. He stopped. He set aside an entire day just to delight in his world.

But notice what else God did: he "blessed the seventh day and made it holy." Two things worth noting here.

First, the Sabbath is "blessed." In the *Genesis* story, three things are blessed by God.

To start with, God blessed the animal kingdom with an invocation: "Be fruitful and multiply."[17]

Then he blessed humanity the same way: "Be fruitful and multiply."[18]

And *then* God blessed the Sabbath.

Wait, so God blessed animals, humans, and then . . . a *day*?

Mmm.

What does that mean?

It means that the Sabbath—just like an animal or a human being—has the life-giving capacity to procreate. To fill the world up with more life.

Life is tiring. (Case in point, most likely you read that line and sighed . . .) You get to the end of the week, and even if you love your job, still you're worn down on every level—emotionally, even spiritually. The Sabbath is how we fill our souls back up with life.

Recently I read a survey done by a doctor who cited the happiest people on earth. Near the top of the list was a group of Christians called Seventh-day Adventists, who are religious, literally, about the Sabbath. This doctor noted that they lived ten years longer than the average American.[19] I did the math: if I Sabbath every seven days, it adds up to—wait for it—*ten years* over a lifetime. Almost exactly. So when I say the Sabbath is life giving, that's not empty rhetoric. If this study is to be believed, every day you Sabbath, you're (statistically and scientifically) likely to get back an elongated life.[20]

From now on, I'm Sabbathing three days a week . . .

And not only will you live longer; even more importantly you'll live *better.*

So first, the Sabbath is "blessed."

Secondly, it's "holy."

Have you ever thought about that? How a day could be called "holy"?

This would have been jarring to the original audience. In the ancient Near East, the gods were found in the world of space, not of time. They were found in a holy temple or on a holy mountain or at a holy shrine. But *this* God—the one, true

Creator God—is found not in a place but in a day. If you want to go and meet with this God, you don't have to make pilgrimage to Mecca or Varanasi or Stonehenge. You just have to set aside a day of the week to Shabbat, stop long enough to experience him.

So there is a day that is *blessed* and *holy.* A rhythm in creation. Six and one. And when we tap into this rhythm, we experience health and life.

But when we fight this rhythm—ignore it, suppress it, push past it, bully it, make excuses, look for a way to get out of it—we reap the consequences.

Consider the mind: we grow mentally lethargic, numb, uncreative, distracted, restless. Emotional unhealth becomes our new normal. Irritability, anger, cynicism, and its twin, sarcasm, overwhelm our defenses and take control of our dispositions.

Or consider the body: we get tired and worn out; our immune systems start to falter, miss a step. *Another* cold. It's like our nervous systems are trying to get our attention.

Yet we push on. Until, inevitably, we crash. Something in our minds or bodies gives out, and we end up flat on our backs. I have my story; I told most of it at the beginning of this book, but I left out the part about my being a type A workaholic, running off ambition (or what do we call it now, *drive*?), with no clue how to rest. I had a weekly day off, sure, but I spent it catching up on all the work I never got paid for (bills, the yard, etc.), as well as things like shopping and entertainment.

Sabbath wasn't even in my vocabulary, much less my vernacular. But we all come to Sabbath, voluntarily or involuntarily. Eventually the grain of the universe caught up with me, and I crashed, *hard*. My sabbatical was like playing catch-up on a decade of missed Sabbaths, come to collect with interest.

I'm guessing you have a story too.

If not, *you will*. Sabbath is coming for you, whether as delight or discipline.

Maybe that's why God eventually has to *command* the Sabbath. Does that strike you as odd? It's like commanding ice cream or live music or beach days. You would think we'd all be chomping at the bit to practice the Sabbath. But apparently there's something about the human condition that makes us want to hurry our way through life as fast as we possibly can, to rebel against the limitations of time itself. Due to our immaturity, dysfunction, and addiction, God has to command his people to do something deeply life giving—rest.

There are a number of Sabbath commands in the Bible. Let me show you the two most important ones.

Command one: Sabbath as rest and worship

Setting: Israel was camped around Mount Sinai. Fresh out of Egypt. They were about to become "a holy nation,"[21] the people of God. But first things first; they needed a manifesto for how to live in the new reality. So God laid out the Ten Commandments, of ACLU courthouse fame. And one command was longer than all the rest. *Way* longer. If you were to configure the Ten Commandments as a pie chart, this one would take up over 30 percent of the pie. And what was the command?

> Remember the Sabbath day by keeping it holy.[22]

I love the opening word, "Remember." It's easy to forget there is a day that's blessed and holy. Easy to get sucked into the life of speed, to let the pace of your life ramp up to a notch shy of insanity. To forget: Creator (not me), creation (me).

Remember that life as it comes to us is a gift.

Remember to take time to delight in it as an act of grateful worship.

Remember to be present to the moment and its joy.

Humans are prone to amnesia, so God commands us to remember.

Then God said this:

> Six days you shall labor and do all your work, but the seventh day is a sabbath to the LORD your God.[23]

Notice that key line: "a sabbath to the LORD." That can also be translated as "set apart for the LORD" or "dedicated to the LORD."

So the Sabbath isn't just a day for rest; it's also a day for worship. By *worship* I don't necessarily mean singing at church (though that's a great example); I mean whole-life orientation toward God.

Take note because this next line is crucial: *the Sabbath isn't the same thing as a day off.*

What's the difference?

Eugene Peterson had a name for a day off; he called it a "bastard Sabbath."**24** The illegitimate child of the seventh day and Western culture. On a day off you don't work for your employer (in theory). But you still work. You run errands, catch up around your house or apartment, pay the bills, make an IKEA run (there goes four hours . . .). And you play! You see a movie, kick the soccer ball with friends, go shopping, cycle through the city. And that's great stuff, all of it. I love my day off. But those activities don't make a Sabbath.

On the Sabbath all we do is *rest* and *worship.*

When I Sabbath, I run each activity through this twin grid: Is this rest and worship? If the answer is "No," or "Kind of, but not really," or "Umm . . . ," then I simply hold off. There are six other days for that. What's the rush? After all, I'm not in a hurry . . .

And notice how easy and free and spacious and non-legalistic this command is. "Rest" and "worship" are broad categories. Plenty of room for interpretation based on your Myers-Briggs type or stage of life. There's no formula or checklist or schedule. Sabbath will look very different for, say, a thirty-something introverted pastor raising a family in a busy city, like me, than for a twenty-year-old single girl living in a college dorm or empty nesters living on a farm. That's great. You do you. The important thing is to set aside a day for nothing but *rest* and *worship.*

Often people hear "worship" and assume that means singing Bethel songs all day while reading the Bible and practicing intercessory prayer. That's all great stuff. But I mean worship in the wide, holistic sense of the word. Expand your list of the spiritual disciplines to include eating a burrito on the patio or drinking a bottle of wine with your friends over a long, lazy dinner or walking on the beach with your lover or best friend—anything to index your heart toward grateful recognition of God's reality and goodness.

Then the command ended with the why, the driving motivation behind the Sabbath:

> For in six days the LORD made the heavens and the earth, the sea, and all that is in them, but he rested on the seventh day. Therefore the LORD blessed the Sabbath day and made it holy.[25]

The Sabbath is the only one of the Ten Commandments with a "why" behind it. God doesn't say, "Don't murder, and here's why it's bad . . ." Or, "Don't steal, and here's why it's not a good idea." But for Sabbath, God goes back to the *Genesis* story, calling his people into the "rhythms of grace."

In fact, I find it fascinating that the Sabbath is the only "spiritual discipline" that makes it into the Ten Commandments.

Not church or Bible reading, not even prayer. Sabbath is the anchor discipline of the people of God. So crucial that God lovingly commands us to remember to rest.

That's command one. Let's do another.

Command two: Sabbath as resistance

Setting: Israel on the edge of the Jordan River, a stone's throw from Canaan. It had been forty years since Mount Sinai. A few things went horribly wrong, and Israel hit a forty-year delay. As a result, Moses had to give the Ten Commandments *again,* to the next generation. Most of them weren't at Mount Sinai, or if they were, they were too young to remember. So it was time for a refresher course. But in Moses's second edition, there's a subtle shift. It's easy to miss, so pay close attention:

> Observe the Sabbath day by keeping it holy, as the LORD your God has commanded you. Six days you shall labor and do all your work, but the seventh day is a sabbath to the LORD your God.[26]

Did you catch it? Yeah, the first word is different. Instead of "remember" the Sabbath, Moses says to "observe" it.

Meaning what, exactly?

Think of how we observe a holiday like Christmas or Easter. We gear up for it, plan out the day in advance, do all we can to make it special, approach it with anticipation. The Sabbath is like that: a holiday every week, but without all the stress and family drama. A once-a-week celebration of all that is good in God's world.

Other than that, the command was pretty much the same, until you get to the end, where it's been edited, this time radically so:

> Remember that you were slaves in Egypt and that the LORD your God brought you out of there with a mighty hand and an outstretched arm. Therefore the LORD your God has commanded you to observe the Sabbath day.[27]

Whoa . . .

That's not a minor tweak; that's a totally different rationale behind the command.

What the heck was Moses up to?

Let me parse it out for you.

In Exodus the Sabbath command is grounded in the creation story. In the rhythm that God built into the world. A rhythm we tap into for emotional health and spiritual life. That's the reason to Sabbath.

But in Deuteronomy the command is grounded in the exodus story. In Israel's freedom from slavery to Pharaoh and his empire. That's a whole *other* reason to Sabbath.

Why the change?

Well, this was the first generation to grow up in freedom. Their parents were slaves. And their grandparents. And their *great*-grandparents. Slaves to an empire that had been devouring human beings, one brick, one pyramid, one edifice at a time, for centuries. An empire with an appetite so ravenous that they had to build "store cities"[28] just to store all their extra stuff. An empire driven by lust for *more*.

And Egypt, like every empire since, was an economic system built on the backs of the oppressed. To get to the lavish, opulent luxury of a pharaoh, you need cheap labor. You need slaves grinding their bodies into the ground until there's nothing left but ash and dust.

Slaves don't get a Sabbath. They don't even get a day off. They work all day, every day, until they die. Slaves are sub-human. A line item on a spreadsheet. Bought and sold like a commodity, a means to whatever end the rich and powerful see fit. All that matters is the bottom line.

And Egypt, my friends, is alive and well.

We live in the thick of it.

We live in a culture of *more.* A culture of gaping, unquench-able lust. For everything. Lust for *more* food, *more* drink, *more* clothes, *more* devices, *more* apps, *more* things, *more* square footage, *more* experiences, *more* stamps on the passport—*more.*

We have so much crap we don't need; we, like Egypt, have to build our own supply cities. We call them storage units, and they are a $38 *billion* industry in the US alone,[29] taking up 2.3 billion square feet, enough for every single American to have over seven square feet to themselves.[30] Meaning, we could practically house our entire nation—*in our storage units.*

Pharaoh would love the USofA.

Just like Egypt, we're an empire built on the oppression of the poor. In America's case (and many other nations), literally. What's more, we've found a way to do slavery guilt-free. We like to think slavery ended in 1865, but the reality is, we just moved it overseas. Out of (our) sight; out of mind. There are twenty-eight million slaves in the world today, more than were *ever* trafficked in the transcontinental slave trade of the eighteenth century.[31] The odds are, your home or apartment is full of stuff they've produced: a T-shirt, a pair of kicks, that clock on the wall, those bananas.

In fact, when economists draw up an image of our global economic system, they draw a pyramid. Some even call it the "Global Wealth Pyramid."

Notice, at the top is 0.7 percent of humanity, weighing in with 45.9 percent of the world's wealth. Those *crazy* rich people who, you know, drive a car, own a computer, have more than one pair of shoes (and possibly are reading this book over a latte that cost five dollars).

At the bottom? A little over 70 percent of our world, with a meager 2.7 percent of our wealth.[32] The vast swath of people in Southeast Asia and all through Africa. The people who make our socks and shoes, our smartphones and our Star

Global wealth pyramid#

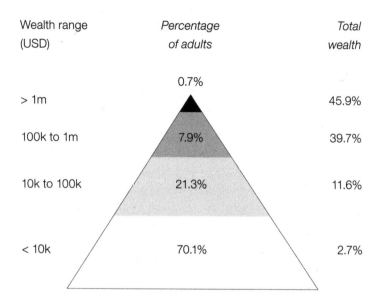

Wealth range (USD)	Percentage of adults	Total wealth
	0.7%	
> 1m		45.9%
100k to 1m	7.9%	39.7%
10k to 100k	21.3%	11.6%
< 10k	70.1%	2.7%

Wars lunch boxes. Many of them working seven days a week, twelve hours a day, in the sweltering heat of a factory in Vietnam or the cold of a cotton field in Uzbekistan, just to survive. Many against their will. Still under the boot of empire.

The odds are, if you're reading this book, you're near the top, not the bottom. That's the tricky thing about Egypt. It's hell if you're a slave, but it's not half bad if you're an American.

I mean, Egyptian.

Now, what does any of this have to do with the Sabbath?

So much.

Sabbath, as the Old Testament scholar Walter Brueggemann so famously said, is "an act of resistance."[33] It's an act of rebellion against Pharaoh and his empire. An insurgency and insurrection against the "isms" of the Western world—globalism, capitalism, materialism, all of which sound nice but quickly make slaves of the rich and the poor. Sabbath is a way to stay free and make sure you never get sucked back into slavery or, *worse,* become the slave driver yourself.

My friend A. J. calls it "scheduled social justice." Often, when I hear about overwhelming injustice in the world or even the growing socioeconomic disparity in my own country, I'm deeply troubled and think, *What in the world can I do?* Well, one thing I can do is do nothing, one day a week.

Can you imagine what would happen to our society if all commerce stopped once a week? If 24-7 stores went 24-6? Websites stopped receiving orders. Amazon warehouses closed for a day. Restaurants powered off the oven. Can you imagine what that would do for the poor in our cities? Creating space for them to rest and spend time with loved ones? Not to mention what it would do for the rest of us. If only we could go an entire day without buying anything.

We can. A few Christian-owned businesses have already taken this courageous step to close their stores and websites on Sundays (for which they are regularly mocked), and while you or I might not head a corporation, by practicing Sabbath, we can still play our small part toward justice in the world.

Sabbath is a way of saying, "Enough." Buying things isn't

always bad, but most of us have more than enough to enjoy a rich and satisfying life. As the psalmist said, "I lack nothing."[34]

That's why under the Torah all buying and selling was off-limits for the Sabbath. This wasn't a legalistic rule from the Old Covenant that we're now "free" from. It was a life-giving practice from the way to break our addiction to the West's twin gods: accomplishment and accumulation. Again, accomplishment and accumulation aren't evil in and of themselves, as long as they don't take advantage of the poor (which usually they *do* . . .). But there's a limit. At some point you have to draw a line in the sand and say, "I'm good. I don't need *another* pair of shoes, *another* decorator item for my bookshelf, *another* toy for my garage, *another* day at the spa."

I have enough.

What I really need is *time* to enjoy what I already have, with God.

The Sabbath is like a guerrilla warfare tactic. If you want to break free from the oppressive yoke of Egypt's taskmaster and its restless, relentless lust for more, just take a day each week and *stick it to the man.* Don't buy. Don't sell. Don't shop. Don't surf the web. Don't read a magazine: ooh, that bathtub would be nice upstairs . . . Just put all that away and *enjoy.* Drink deeply from the well of ordinary life: a meal with friends, time with family, a walk in the forest, afternoon tea. Above all, slow down long enough to enjoy life with God, who offers everything that materialism promises but can never deliver on—namely, contentment.

In the words of Ronald Rolheiser, who I feel should get royalties on this book:

> So much of our unhappiness comes from comparing our lives, our friendships, our loves, our commitments, our duties, our bodies and our sexuality to some idealized and non-Christian vision of things which falsely assures us that there is a heaven on earth.
>
> When that happens, and it does, our tensions begin to drive us mad, in this case to a cancerous restlessness.[35]

Oh man, that phrase, "cancerous restlessness." He continued:

> True restfulness, though, is a form of awareness, a way of being in life. It is living ordinary life with a sense of ease, gratitude, appreciation, peace and prayer. We are restful when ordinary life is enough.[36]

So what will it be? A "cancerous restlessness" that's as old as Pharaoh? Always comparing your life to the next person's? Itching for the next purchase to ratchet your way to the top? Or a healing contentment from an unhurried, unharried life?

What if ordinary life is enough?

A governor on the speed of life

Speaking of a cancerous restlessness and buying things we don't need, when T and I were first married, back in the glory days of DINK (double income, no kids), she bought me a motorcycle for Christmas.

Yes, the wifery is awesome.

So naturally, I had to reciprocate. A few months later, for our anniversary, I bought her a Vespa. Brand-new, sky blue, happiness on wheels.

I had to get a motorcycle endorsement on my license before I could even test-drive my bike, but not T. Her Vespa had this device called a "governor" on it. You know what that is? I didn't. Turns out it's a little cap on the engine that keeps it from going over fifty miles per hour. Under Oregon law, as long as a moped can't go over fifty, you don't need a motor-cycle endorsement.

You see where this is going.

The Sabbath is like a governor on the speed of life.

All week long we work, we play, we cook, we clean, we shop, we exercise, we answer text messages, we inhabit the modern world, but finally we hit a limit. On the Sabbath, we slow down; more than that, we come to a full stop.

One of the surprising things I learned when I began to practice Sabbath is that to really enjoy the seventh day, you have to slow down the *other* six days. You can't go ninety miles per hour all week, running the pedal to the floor, harrowing your soul to the bone for six days straight, and then expect to slam on the brakes for Sabbath and immediately feel zen awesome. You have to find the rhythm. As we used to say when I played in indie rock bands, "Find the pocket."

Because the Sabbath isn't just a twenty-four-hour time slot in your weekly schedule; it's a *spirit* of restfulness that goes with you throughout your week. A way of living with "ease, gratitude, appreciation, peace and prayer." A way of working from rest, not for rest, with nothing to prove. A way of bearing fruit from abiding, not ambition.

As Brueggemann said so eloquently:

> People who keep Sabbath live all seven days differently.[37]

That's why the Sabbath is on day seven, not day three or four. It's not a break in the week to rest up so we can get back to what really matters: work. It's the climax, the apogee, what the entire week has been leading up to.

If you aren't practicing the Sabbath, you're missing out on the best day of the week, bar none.

So.

Deep breath.

Almost done.

To wind down this chapter, let me just speak from the heart. I deeply enjoy the practice of Sabbath. For me it's not a legalistic hangover from some fundamentalist shtick but a practice from the way of Jesus, a delivery system for *life*.

There are all sorts of debate and controversy about whether we still have to keep the Sabbath as followers of Jesus. I'm in a minority that thinks we do. It's one of the Ten Commandments, after all, and Jesus did absolutely nothing to annul it. Yes, the early church moved it to Sunday, but up until the 1950s, Sunday was "the Lord's day," and that meant a lot more than church for two hours; it meant an entire day of rest. But honestly? I wouldn't really care if I don't have to keep the Sabbath anymore. I *want* to keep the Sabbath. Even if the Sabbath is no longer a binding command, it's still the grain of the universe. It's a gift—and one I want to open and enjoy.

Nine times out of ten, Sabbath is the best day of my week, no exaggeration. Every Friday night, after Sabbath dinner, we bake a giant cookie in a cast-iron pan, a full square foot of chocolate yumminess. Then we dump a carton of ice cream on the top, let it melt a little, and eat it all straight out of the pan—it's some kind of symbolic nod to both our unity as a family and our collective love of sugar. As we indulge, we go around the table and share our highlight of the week. I feel like a broken record because I almost always say, "Last Sabbath!" Something spectacular usually has to go down to beat out the previous week's Sabbath for joy.

The Sabbath is the day I feel most connected to God. Most connected to my wife and family. To my own soul. It's the day I feel most *awake* and yet most at peace. The day I expect joy. The day that sets the tone for my entire week.

On Wednesday or Thursday I find myself saying under my breath, "I can do this," because *I know the Sabbath is coming.*

On Sunday or Monday I find myself thinking, *I can do this because I'm living off the Sabbath.*

When I remember my life before the Sabbath, I shudder. I never want to go back to Egypt. Never want to become slave or slave driver again. I'm *free.* I want to stay that way.

And I want you to experience this day of unhurried love and joy and peace.

You know you want it . . .

If your story is anything like mine, Sabbath will take you a little while to master. After all, *Shabbat* is a verb. It's something you do. A practice, a skill you hone. It took years of trial and error for me. As our kids age into their teens, our practice continues to adapt and iterate.

Point being: this practice is *so* foreign and alien to our culture, even our church culture, that it might take you a while to dial it in. That's okay.

Remember, you're not in a hurry.

To begin, just set aside a day. Clear your schedule. TURN OFF YOUR PHONE. Say a prayer to invite the Holy Spirit to pastor you into his presence. And then? *Rest* and *worship.* In whatever way is life giving for your soul.

My family and I do this every week. Just before sunset on Friday, we finish up all our to-do lists and homework and grocery shopping and responsibilities, power down all our devices (we literally put them all in a box and stow it in a closet), and gather around the table as a family. We open a bottle of wine, light some candles, read a psalm, pray. Then we feast, and we basically don't stop feasting for the next twenty-four hours. It's the Comer way! And, I might add, the Jesus way. We sleep in Saturday morning. Drink coffee. Read our Bibles. Pray more. Spend time together. Talk. Laugh. In summer, walk to the park. In winter, make a fire. Get lost in good novels on the couch. Cuddle. Nap. (The Jews even have a name for the Sabbath nap—the *Shabbat shluf!* We shluf hard on Sabbath.) Make love.

Honestly, I spend a lot of time just sitting by the window, being. It's like a less stressful Christmas every week.

And something happens about halfway through the day, something hard to put language to. It's like my soul catches up to my body. Like some deep part of me that got beat up and drowned out by meetings and email and Twitter and relational conflict and the difficulty of life comes back to the surface of my heart.

I feel free.

Free from the need to do more, get more, *be* more. Free from the spirit—the evil, demonic spirit—of restlessness that enslaves our society. I feel another spirit, the *Holy* Spirit, of restful calm settle over my whole person. And I find that my ordinary life is enough.

And on Saturday evening when I turn my phone back on and reenter the modern world, I do so *slowly*. And, wow, does that ever feel good.

Simplicity

Let's start out with a few sayings of Jesus that, if we're honest, most of us disagree with or at least dislike.

> Watch out! Be on your guard against all kinds of greed; life does not consist in an abundance of possessions.[1]

Or how about this one?

> Sell your possessions and give to the poor.[2]

Wait, what about saving for retirement? Don't you know about the social security crisis? Medicare? This sounds irresponsible.

> Do not worry about your life, what you will eat or drink; or about your body, what you will wear. Is not life more

than food, and the body more than clothes? . . . Seek first [God's] kingdom.³

Okay, you lost me; that's *exactly* what I worry about. Money to pay the bills. Do you have any idea what rent is in my city? Not to mention my student loans. Are you expecting me to just sit around and pray all day long?

The worries of this life, the deceitfulness of wealth and the desires for other things come in and choke the word, making it unfruitful.⁴

You're saying that wealth is by nature "deceitful"? A personified con artist? That it has a suffocating effect on the soil of my heart, choking out the life of the kingdom?

Again I tell you, it is easier for a camel to go through the eye of a needle than for someone who is rich to enter the kingdom of God.⁵

You're saying wealth makes it *harder* to experience the life of God's reign? Not easier? That does not compute. The more money I have, the better my life seems.

Confused?

If these sayings of Jesus sound crazy to you, well, you're not alone. They do to most of us in the West. When I first started to take Jesus seriously as a teacher (not just as a savior), it was his vision of the role of wealth in the good life that was most jarring to me. Honestly, it took me years to even agree with him.

If you're not on board with Jesus' view of money, it could be that you, like many Christians in the West (myself included until quite recently and with frequent relapses), don't actually believe the gospel of the kingdom—the good news that the life you've always wanted is fully available to you right where you are through Jesus. Through him you have access to the Father's loving presence. Nothing—not your income level or stage of life or health or relational status—*nothing* is standing between you and the "life that is truly life."[6]

It could be that you believe *another* gospel. Another vision of what the good life is and how you obtain it.

Let's call it "the gospel of America."

(For those of you outside America, I apologize; just roll with it.)

This gospel makes the exact opposite claim. In a nutshell: the more you have, the happier you will be.

Get that new dress or pair of shoes or golf club or geometric potted cactus, and naturally you'll be happier.

Trade your car in for the new model; it has LED lights around the logo.

Nab the bigger, better home or condo or apartment, and make sure you furnish it with the latest design trend, preferably from Sweden or Australia.

Work your way up the ladder, throw an elbow if you have to, but get the promotion, the raise, the bonus.

If and when you do, you'll be happier. Duh. Everybody knows that. Happiness is out there; it's just one PayPal click or outfit or gadget or car payment or mortgage away. Out of reach, yes. But barely. I'm *almost* there. I can feel it.

But let me say what you all know: the carrot dangling in front of our noses is attached to a stick.

The French sociologist Jean Baudrillard has made the point that in the Western world, materialism has become the new, dominant system of meaning.[7] He argues atheism hasn't replaced cultural Christianity; shopping has.

We now get our meaning in life from what we consume.

We even get our identity from the things we buy (or sell). Most of us would never admit it, but a lot of us believe the saying "I am what I buy." Or more realistically, "I am what I wear." Or the brand of my phone. Or the car I drive or the neighborhood I live in or the gadget I flaunt.

For a lot of people, things aren't just *things;* they are identities.

Shopping is now the number one leisure activity in America, usurping the place previously held by religion. Amazon.com is the new temple. The Visa statement is the new altar. Double-clicking is the new liturgy. Lifestyle bloggers are the priests and priestesses. Money is the new god.

There's a reason the only other god Jesus ever called out by name was Mammon—the god of money.[8] Because it's a bad god and a lousy religion.

The rise of a lie

It hasn't always been this way, even in America. Yes, our nation is a social experiment built around the pursuit of happiness. But it wasn't until quite recently that we redefined happiness as making lots of money and owning lots of stuff.

Only a century ago (a blip on the history time line), 90 percent of Americans were farmers. Life was hard, yes, but simpler too. We mostly lived off the land and traded with our neighbors for anything else we needed. Money was rarely even used. And most of the things we owned fell into the category of needs, not wants.

Today only 2 percent of Americans work in agriculture. The last century has radically reshaped the American economy. It started with urbanization and its twin, industrialization. People moved to cities by the droves for jobs, where goods were produced in mass. The two world wars in turn created what President Eisenhower later dubbed "the military-industrial complex," and once the tumult of war calmed down, the power brokers of the day had to find a way to keep all those factories open and people employed. Tank factories were repurposed to make T-shirts.

I'm not much of a conspiracy theorist, but it's an open secret that after the war, the tycoons of big business, the shadow politicians of DC, and the "mad men" of New York City conspired to remake the American economy. Their agenda? To create an entire economy (and, with it, culture) out of consumerism. To get the children of a bunch of simple farmers to spend their time and money buying up the latest thing, hot off the assembly line. It was the "thingification" of American society.

One Wall Street banker said this:

> We must shift America from a needs to a desires culture. . . . People must be trained to desire, to want new things, even before the old have been entirely consumed. We must shape a new mentality. Man's desires must overshadow his needs.[9]

Sound like an evil genius from an Orwellian sci-fi movie? Nah. That was Paul Mazur of Lehman Brothers.

E. S. Cowdrick, a pioneer of "industrial relations," called it "the new economic gospel of consumption." Note his language: "gospel."

And tragically, their evil plan worked. Perfectly.

In 1927 one journalist observed this about America:

> A change has come over our democracy. It is called consumptionism. The American citizen's first importance to his country is now no longer that of citizen but that of consumer.[10]

Fast-forward to today: our "consumer" economy is now built

around people spending money they don't have on things they don't need. And we've all heard how our apartments and homes are twice the size they were in the '50s, while our families are half the size.[11]

One of my most vivid memories is 9/11. I still remember that morning, hearing the news. On West Coast time it was pretty early, and I spent most of the day in shock.

But I also remember President Bush's speech to the nation a few weeks later. You remember what the leader of the free world encouraged us to do to get our nation back on track?

Go shopping.

That's a bit cynical of an interpretation, but at one point in the speech, he warned against terrorists "frightening our nation to the point where . . . people don't shop."[12]

God forbid that a tragedy like 9/11 keep us from hitting up the mall for a new pair of Nikes.

Even as a teenager that sounded bizarre to me.

But the crazy thing is, that's exactly what we did. In fact, we bought so much stuff and borrowed so much money to do it that our entire economy crashed only a few years later. (Yes, that's an oversimplification, but not by a lot.) I say this not to dishonor a president for a slip of the tongue, but to situate it in a larger cultural trend.

Because we grew up in a cultural milieu where this was

normal and we're educated to believe we're rational, auto-nomous selves, it's easy to forget that most advertising is a form of propaganda, one that plays not to our pre-frontal cortex but to a deeper, less logical part of us. Prior to World War II, advertising was nothing like it is today. All it really did was tell you why one product was better than another. The messages from advertising were about quality, longevity, necessity.

Here are a few examples from a couple of centuries ago:

> Simplicity. Durability. Speed. Visible Writing. Franklin Typewriter.

> Dr. Warner's Celebrated Coraline Corsets. They are boned with Coraline, which is the only material used for Corsets that can be guaranteed not to wrinkle nor break.

> Tired? Then drink Coca-Cola. It relieves exhaustion.[13]

Notice: absolutely nothing about how a product will make you happy.

But the war changed everything.

Advertising as we now know it started not on Madison Avenue but in another city: Berlin. With another group of power brokers: the Nazis. They took the ideas of an Austrian psychotherapist named Freud, then unknown in America, and used them to manipulate the masses. Freud was one of the first modern thinkers to point out that human beings aren't nearly as rational or autonomous as we like to think. We constantly make irrational decisions based on what he called our "unconscious drives" (similar to what the New Testament calls "the flesh"). We are far more emotionally tricked and desire driven than we care to admit.

The Nazis picked up Freud's ideas (which was ironic, seeing as he was Jewish) and used them to shape their propaganda machine. They appealed not to reason but to Germany's "unconscious drives." Hitler was a master of fanning the two most basic human emotions: I want, and I fear.

After the war, it was actually Freud's nephew, Edward Bernays, who first used Freud's ideas in America. An intelligence officer during the war, he found himself in need of a job. His theory was that if the Nazis could manipulate people in wartime, then surely business owners and politicians could manipulate people in peacetime. He called his new idea "public relations" and became the so-called "father of American advertising."[14]

Never heard of him? Most haven't. He predicted as much in his book *Propaganda:*

> The conscious and intelligent manipulation of the orga-nized habits and opinions of the masses is an important element in democratic society. Those who manipulate this unseen mechanism of society constitute *an invisible government which is the true ruling power of our country.*
> We are governed, our minds are molded, our tastes formed, our ideas suggested, largely by men we have never heard of. . . . In almost every act of our daily

lives . . . *we are dominated by the relatively small number of persons . . . who pull the wires which control the public mind.*[15]

My point with this little history jaunt is to remind us: advertising *is* propaganda. It might not be trying to get you to kill Jews, Gypsies, and LGBTQ people, but it is a multibillion-dollar industry that is intentionally designed to lie to you—to get you to believe that if you will only buy this or that product, *then* you will be happy. Or at least happ*ier*.

To do this it has to bend over backward to make us think our wants are actually needs. Those four thousand ads we see a day have been intentionally designed to stoke the fire of desire in our bellies.[16]

Before any of this even started, Mark Twain perceptively noted, "Civilization is the limitless multiplication of unnecessary necessities."[17] Nail on the head, as always. As Western wealth and technology continue to rise, many psychologists point out that our happiness is not increasing at pace. In fact, some studies indicate that as a nation's wealth goes up, its happiness goes down. Or at least levels off. Something about the human psyche quickly adapts to a new normal. Things we categorize as "needs"—a car, a telephone, a daily multivitamin, electricity, running water—didn't even exist until recently, and yet many people were quite happy without them.

The journalist Gregg Easterbrook, in his book *The Progress Paradox: How Life Gets Better While People Feel Worse,* noted this:

Adjusting for population growth, ten times as many people in the Western nations today suffer from "unipolar" depression, or unremitting bad feelings without a specific cause, than did half a century ago. Americans and Europeans have ever more of everything except happiness.[18]

So what to do? Go back to a hole in the backyard as our toilet? Give up running water? Burn our debit cards? No, that wouldn't fix the problem. Because the problem isn't stuff. It's that (1) we put no limit on stuff due to our insatiable human desire for *more*. And (2) we think we need all sorts of things to be happy when, in actuality, we need very few.

Jesus and the writers of the New Testament put the number of our material needs at a whopping two things: food and clothing.

> If we have food and clothing, we will be content with that.[19]

Now, Jesus and his friends lived in and around the Mediterranean Sea, where it's warm and dry. I live in the Pacific Northwest, where it's cold and wet half the year, so I would add one more to the list: shelter.

But even the thought of living by that expanded list—food, clothing, and shelter—sounds *crazy* to most of us.

What if the only material things we need to live rich and satisfying lives are food to eat, clothing on our backs, and a place to live? If you doubt your ability to live that simply and thrive, you're not alone.

The propaganda machine is working like a charm. Most of us believe the lie: more money and more stuff equal more happiness.

And like all the most dangerous lies, it's a half-truth. More money does make you happier—if you're *poor.* I hate the way some idealistic Christians (who aren't poor) glamorize poverty. It's horrible. Lifting people out of poverty will make them happier, but only up to a point.

And we now know exactly what that point is: $75,000.

The truth about lies

In a landmark study out of Princeton University, two great minds collaborated on a nationwide research project. Dr. Daniel Kahneman, a Nobel Prize–winning psychologist, and Dr. Angus Deaton, a well-respected economist, spent months poring over the data from 450,000 Gallup surveys and concluded that your overall well-being does rise with your income, but only to a point. After that you either plateau or, worse, decline.

Here's Deaton in his own words:

> No matter where you live, your emotional well-being is as good as it's going to get at $75,000 . . . and money's not going to make it any better beyond that point. It's like you

hit some sort of ceiling, and you can't get emotional well-being much higher just by having more money.

Now, that number is a national average. It would be much less for, say, a single college kid living in Sarasota Springs than for a family of five living in San Francisco. Jennifer Robison, in her summary of Kahneman's and Deaton's research, says that it's "true, $75,000 won't go very far in big cities . . . and it makes sense that a high cost of living will make even large sums feel puny." However, the study still "indicates that $75,000 is the limit even in large expensive cities."[20]

Turns out: once you reach what most Westerners classify as a middle-class life, money and stuff just can't deliver what they promise—happiness.

As the oil tycoon John Rockefeller so famously said when asked how much money is "enough": "Just a little bit more."

To drill down, the lie is this: more money (and, with it, stuff) will make you happier.

The truth? Poverty is really hard and a middle-class life is a real gift, but after that it's the law of diminishing returns. In fact, more money might just be "mo problems." But wherever you fall in the socioeconomic stratum, the most important things in life aren't things at all; they are relationships with family, friends, and, above all, God.

You see how upside down our culture's message about money and stuff is? Richard Foster called our culture's view of things "psychotic" in that it has completely lost touch with reality. He wisely observed, "We in the West are guinea pigs in one huge economic experiment in consumption."[21]

In my opinion, the wait is over and the verdict is in: time *is* telling the catastrophic damage that materialism is doing to the soul of our society. This lie we all believe is wreaking havoc on our emotional health and spiritual lives. One cultural commentator called it "affluenza."[22] It's like a disease promising to make us happy for $49.99, while in fact it's a man in the shadows pulling our strings and stealing our money and, with it, our joy.

This all reminds me of a line from Psalm 39: "In vain they rush about, heaping up wealth without knowing whose it will finally be."[23]

An engine for hurry

One of the many reasons that happiness is dropping in the West even as the Dow is rising is because materialism has sped up our society to a frenetic, untenable pace.

As Alan Fadling insightfully said,

> The drive to possess is an engine for hurry.[24]

Every single thing you buy costs you not only money but also *time.*

Think about it: you buy that motorcycle you've always

dreamed of; that's great. I used to ride. I miss it. Have fun; don't die. But make sure you do the math before you sign on the dotted line. *All* the math. To own a bike costs a lot more than just the $250-per-month payment you can't really afford. It costs you time—you have to work more hours at your job to pay for it. You have to move *faster* through your day to get everything done. You have to keep your bike clean. And maintain it. When it breaks, you have to fix it. And of course, you have to ride it. All of this takes a lot of time. Now, you might be in a season of your life where you have time to burn, and you might decide that riding a motorcycle is a life-giving activity for your soul. Great. I'm not remotely against it. I can vaguely remember a similar season, before kids. But when you run your cost-benefit analysis, don't forget to calculate: you're paying for that experience not only in cash but also in time.

And less time means more *hurry.*

Whether you're into motorcycles, sneakers, or Japanese anime, most of us simply have too much stuff to enjoy life at a healthy, unhurried pace.

Remember those predictions from the Nixon era that by now we'd all be working three or four hours each morning and playing golf in the afternoon while the robots made our living for us? What happened? Well, part of the story is that we chose money and stuff over time and freedom. We opted for a new 4K projector for movie night instead of "a life of unhurried serenity and peace and power."[25] Instead of spending money to get time, we opted for the reverse: we spend time to get money.

So.

I have a crazy idea.

You ready?

What if Jesus was *right*?

I mean, what if he actually knew what he was talking about?

We forget, Jesus was the most intelligent teacher to ever live. His teachings aren't just right in some arbitrary moral sense— they are *good.* That's what morality is—the good and true way to live.

It's a gross mistake to think of Jesus' teachings as some kind of socially conditioned, arbitrary law like the speed limit—who says it has to be forty-five miles per hour? Why not fifty-five? What if I have a brand-new Tesla?

In reality Jesus' moral teachings aren't arbitrary at all. They are laws, yes. But moral laws are no different from scientific laws like $E = mc^2$ or gravity.[26] *They are statements about how the world actually works.* And if you ignore them, not only do you rupture relationship with God, but you also go against the grain of the universe he created. Cue the splinters.

So many of Jesus' teachings—especially on money and stuff— were just telling stories about the way the world actually *is.*

It is more blessed to give than to receive.[27]

Notice: that's not a command, much less an arbitrary law. It's a counterintuitive observation of the human condition.

You cannot serve both God and money.[28]

Notice, again, not a command. He didn't say, "You *shouldn't* serve both God and money." He said, "You *can't.*"

Life does not consist in an abundance of possessions.[29]

Yet again, he didn't command, "Don't buy more than three pairs of shoes." He just made a statement about the way life actually works. The most important things in life aren't in your closet or your garage or your online portfolio. That's just not where "abundance" is found.

You see what he was doing? He was teaching what's *true.* Whether we believe him or not is another matter. Either way, his ideas about money and stuff correspond to reality. Ours to psychopathy.

Now for a bit of confession. I grew up reading the Bible all the way through every year, and around September I would get to Jesus' teachings. They say something like 25 percent of Jesus' teachings are on money and stuff. Basically, none of them are positive. Wherever the "prosperity gospel" came from, it didn't come from Jesus. And honestly, when I read his teachings on money, I cringed. They sounded *horrible.* Right up there with fasting and celibacy. Like, if I were to live those teachings, it would suck the joy right out of life.

Like many of my fellow Americans, I did not believe the gospel of the kingdom. I didn't yet trust (that's what it means to believe) that Jesus was a master teacher, an astute observer of the human condition, and that his teachings were not just right but were *the best way to live.*

It wasn't until I started to dabble in minimalism (more on that in a bit) and it immediately unleashed a flood of joy and peace in my life that I started to take Jesus' teachings on money seriously. I can still remember the afternoon where it hit me like a freight train: Jesus was *right.*

Daaaaang . . .

This is actually a better, freer way to live.

At the time this was a shockingly virgin idea for me, full confession.

Then I started to question all the assumptions of my culture. I took Tyler Durden's advice: "Reject the basic assumptions of civilization, especially the importance of material possessions." (And, yes, that was a quote from *Fight Club*.)[30]

I started asking myself questions the secret police of advertising would disappear me for:

- What if the formula "more stuff equals more happiness" is bad math?

- What if more stuff often just equals more *stress*? More hours at the office, more debt, more years working in a job I don't feel called to, more time wasted cleaning and maintaining and fixing and playing with and organizing and reorganizing and updating all that junk I don't even need.

- What if more stuff actually equals *less* of what matters most? Less time. Less financial freedom. Less generosity, which according to Jesus is where the real joy is. Less peace, as I hurry my way through the mall parking lot. Less focus on what life is actually about. Less mental real estate for creativity. Less relationships. Less margin. Less prayer. Less of what I actually ache for?

- What if I were to reject my culture's messaging as a half-truth at best, if not a full-on lie, and live into another message? Another gospel?

Jesus and the "evil" eye

For all the flack that pastors get for talking about money too much (a lot of which is well deserved), Jesus actually had a ton to say on the subject.

Let's take a closer look at Matthew 6 and his most in-depth teaching on the subject in the so-called Sermon on the Mount. Interestingly, it takes up about 25 percent of the sermon.

First Jesus said this:

> Do not store up for yourselves treasures on earth, where moths and vermin destroy, and where thieves break in and steal. But store up for yourselves treasures in

heaven, where moths and vermin do not destroy, and where thieves do not break in and steal. For where your treasure is, there your heart will be also.[31]

Basically: don't invest all your time and energy (and money) in things that get old and rust and go out of style and can be snatched from the back of your car if you park too far from the streetlamp. Instead: put your life into things that matter, like your relationship with God and life in his kingdom. Because where you put your resources is where you put your heart. It's the steering wheel to your engine of desire.

Then:

The eye is the lamp of the body. If your eyes are healthy, your whole body will be full of light. But if your eyes are unhealthy, your whole body will be full of darkness. If then the light within you is darkness, how great is that darkness![32]

If you're thinking, *Wait, what does optometry have to do with money?* this is a first-century idiom that's lost on our modern ears. In Jesus' day, if people said you had a "healthy" eye, it had a double meaning. It meant that (1) you were focused and living with a high degree of intentionality in life, and (2) you were generous to the poor. When you looked at the world, you saw those in need and did your best to help out. An "unhealthy" eye (or as the King James Version has it, an "evil" eye) was the exact opposite. When you looked out on the world, you were distracted by all that glitters and lost your focus on what really matters. In turn, you closed your fist to the poor.

Then Jesus took it over the finish line:

> No one can serve two masters. Either you will hate the one and love the other, or you will be devoted to the one and despise the other. You cannot serve both God and money.[33]

Again, cannot, not should not.

For Jesus it's a non-option. You cannot serve God and the system.[34] You simply can't live the freedom way of Jesus *and* get sucked into the overconsumption that is normal in our society. The two are mutually exclusive. You have to pick.

And if you're on the fence about it, as I was for years, the next line from Jesus was the clincher for me:

> Therefore I tell you, do not worry about your life.[35]

Notice how Jesus connected money and stuff to *worry.*

You see that?

The word "therefore" is the key. It ties together three short teachings on money and stuff to one long teaching on worry (go read the end of Matthew 6 for the full version). Basic point? We worry about what we worship. If you worship money, it will eat you alive.

Who wants that?

Basically nobody.

Now we're ready: simplicity

Is there a way off this merry-go-round from Gehenna? A practice from the life and teachings of Jesus to break free of the soul-draining habits of Western materialism and live into the reality of how life actually works?

That's a leading question. Of course there is. This practice is called simplicity, but it goes by a few other names:

> Simple living—that's a bit clearer, which is nice.
>
> Frugality—this is what the monks called it, but that word has lost all positive connotations, so I avoid it.
>
> Minimalism—more recently, this is what a number of bloggers and writers have been calling a secularized version of the ancient practice, updated for the wealthy Western world. I like it.

For this chapter, I'll use simplicity and minimalism interchangeably.

To get started, what exactly *is* it?

Well, let's start with what it's *not.*

First, it's not a style of architecture or design.

A lot of people hear the word "minimalism" and think of a modern home with angular design, high-end furniture, a black-and-white palate, magazinesque neatness, and of course, no kids.

If you have OCD and are a clean-freak, perfectionistic architecture enthusiast like me with an odd taste for monastery meets MoMA, you get excited by that.

Most don't.

But hey, good news: you don't have to be into modern design to be a minimalist. You can dig California-Spanish revival or *Kinfolk*-earthy chic or '80s video-game arcade with a touch of Boba Fett—whatever your style is. That's great.

Secondly, it isn't poverty. It isn't a bare home, an empty closet, a joyless life with no freedom to enjoy material things. The whole goal is exactly the opposite—*more* freedom.

Again: a lot of people hear *minimalism* and think of Steve Jobs's house—an empty living room with nothing but a chair and lamp in it.

(Hey, at least it was an Eames Lounge Chair in walnut. The man had *taste*.)

Minimalism isn't about living with *nothing;* it's about living with *less.*

Thirdly, minimalism isn't about organizing your stuff. Cleaning out the garage every spring. Cleaning out your closet for the ninth time. Making a run to Target to buy twenty plastic bins and a label gun.[36]

God bless Marie Kondo, her work is great, but I would argue that "organizing" is antithetical to minimalism. If you have so much stuff that you have to organize it, box it up, label it, and stack it in a way that cuts down on space, then the odds are you have too much stuff!

(Unless you live in a tiny apartment in San Francisco or New York, in which case you get a pass.)

What if you had only what you needed, and there wasn't anything to organize? There's an idea worth chasing down.

Well, then, what *is* minimalism? Or simplicity, or whatever label you prefer? Here are a few definitions I find helpful.

Joshua Becker, a follower of Jesus and former pastor who now writes about minimalism full time, defined it these ways:

> The intentional promotion of the things we most value and the removal of everything that distracts us from them.[37]

Another fine definition comes from Richard Foster and Mark Scandrette:

> "Simplicity is an inward reality that can be seen in an outward lifestyle"[38] of "choosing to leverage time, money, talents and possessions toward what matters most."[39]

Notice that minimalism isn't just about your money and stuff; it's about your whole life. As Thoreau joyfully said after going off into the woods for a multiyear experiment in simple living:

> Simplicity, simplicity, simplicity! I say, let your affairs be as

two or three, and not a hundred or a thousand. . . . Why should we live with such hurry and waste of life?[40]

See how he connects the dots between simplicity and hurry? Perceptive.

To live this way, we have to pare down *all* our resources, both time and money. As Saint Francis de Sales, bishop of Geneva, once said, "In everything, love simplicity."[41] I love that—in *everything.*

The goal isn't just to declutter your closet or garage but to declutter your *life.* To clear away the myriad of distractions that ratchet up our anxiety, feed us an endless stream of mind-numbing drivel, and anesthetize us to what really matters.

To keep the definitions coming, here are a few one-liners for clutter:

> Anything that does not add value to my life.[42]
>
> Anything that does not "spark joy."[43]
>
> Too much stuff in too small a space, . . . anything that we no longer used or loved, and . . . anything that led to a feeling of disorganization.[44]

The goal here is to live with a high degree of intentionality around what matters most, which, for those of us who apprentice under Jesus, is Jesus himself and his kingdom.

If you're a bit cynical and you're currently thinking, *Isn't this just for rich people?*

Well, yes.

Poor people don't call it simple living; they just call it *living*. They don't read books on minimalism; they pray for justice.

But if you're reading this book, the odds are very high that you're not poor. Again, and with zero guilt trip, to put things in perspective, if you make $25,000 a year or more, you're in the top 10 percent of the world's wealth. And if you make $34,000 a year or more, you're in the top *1 percent*.[45]

Listen to Paul's command to the rich in Ephesus:

> Command those who are rich in this present world not to be arrogant nor to put their hope in wealth, which is so uncertain. . . .
>   Command them to do good, to be rich in good deeds, and to be generous and willing to share.
>   In this way they will lay up treasure for themselves as a firm foundation for the coming age, so that they may take hold of the life that is truly life.[46]

This was Paul riffing on Jesus' teaching from Matthew 6. See the quote in there? And he was saying the same thing Jesus did: simplicity is actually the way we reach out and grasp the "life that is truly life."

I read this verse for years and thought it was about somebody *else*. I know a few rich people; I figured this verse was about them. Not about me. I grew up thoroughly middle class. We had a home, which was a gift, but our vacations were camping or staying at my grandparents' cabin. My

clothing was never name brand. I remember getting merci-
lessly mocked in grade school for my ugly shoes. We rarely
ate out. So I just never thought of myself as wealthy.

I also grew up hopelessly out of touch not only with global
poverty but also with the way that many people, especially
people of color, are living right here in our own country.

But even if I *weren't* rich (which, turns out, I am), I'm not off
the hook; most of Jesus' teachings on money weren't to rich
people. In fact, the majority of his audience was likely poor.

Think about Jesus. Simplicity is a practice that's entirely
based on his life. Myth-busting time: Jesus wasn't nearly as
poor as many people claim. Before he became a rabbi, he
was a tradesman, likely making a living wage. Once he
started teaching full time, he was supported by a group of
wealthy donors (mostly upper-class women) who paid for his
food and travel expenses.[47] He even needed one of his
disciples to manage the budget (of course, that didn't turn
out too well, but . . .). He was friends with both the rich and
the poor, but there are lots of stories about him eating and
drinking at the home of one of his rich friends, so much so
that the gospel writers admit he was accused of being a
"glutton and a drunkard."[48] Even at the cross the Roman
soldiers cast lots for his garments, meaning they were worth
something. John even wrote, "This [under]garment was
seamless, woven in one piece from top to bottom."[49]

In Jesus' life and teaching we see the very same tension that
runs all the way through the library of Scripture: on the one
hand, the world and everything in it are "very good" and

meant to be enjoyed and shared with those in need. On the other hand, too much wealth is dangerous. It has the potential to turn our hearts away from God. When that happens, our greedy, off-kilter hearts wreak havoc not only on our own lives, sabotaging our happiness, but more importantly on others', widening the gap between rich and poor and doing damage to the earth itself.

We see Jesus happily living in that tension. Enjoying a good meal in a friend's home one minute and warning about what money can do to your heart the next.

To be fair, in that tension Jesus clearly sided with minimalism over materialism. No question. As Richard Foster noted, "a carefree unconcern for possessions" is what "marks life in the kingdom."[50] And Jesus put on display this "carefree unconcern" so incredibly well.

To follow Jesus, especially in the Western world, is to live in that same tension between grateful, happy enjoyment of nice, beautiful things, and simplicity. And when in doubt, to err on the side of generous, simple living.

The practice

So, you ready to get started?

One of my favorite things about Jesus as a teacher is how he regularly ended his teachings with small, creative practices to live out his heady ideas about the kingdom of God.[51] Let's do that.

First we'll hit on some principles, then the practice itself. Note: these are principles, not rules; this is about more freedom, not more rules. Here are my top twelve.

1. Before you buy something, ask yourself, What is the true cost of this item?

Back to the motorcycle example: Think about what it will cost to clean, repair, maintain, insure, finance, etc. the item. It's more than just the ticket price. Can you actually afford it? How much time will it cost me to own this? How often will I use it? Will it add value to my life and help me enjoy God and his world even more? Or just distract me from what really matters?

Finally, measure *hurry.* What will this do to the pace of my life? Speed it up or slow it down?

2. Before you buy, ask yourself, By buying this, am I oppressing the poor or harming the earth?

We all know that the level at which Americans consume is doing great harm to the earth. Scientists argue it would take something like five earths for everyone on the planet to live with the same ecological footprint as the average American.[52] Think of something as common as polyester, which is now in a startling 50 percent of our clothes and is non-biodegradable. That cute athletic-wear outfit? It will *always* exist, in a landfill. FOREVER.

Some of us care deeply about environmental issues; others,

not so much. Fine. But the earth isn't the only victim of our overconsumption.

A few years ago I was shocked and deeply disturbed when I learned about the dark underbelly of globalization. I had no clue that a huge chunk of the items in my home and life were made unjustly, if not with full-on human trafficking and child labor.

Take the garment industry for example, which has radically changed since the mad men–era. In the 1960s, 95 percent of our clothes were made in America, and Americans spent on average 10 percent of their annual budget on clothing and owned very few items.

Today only 2 percent of our clothing is made in the US, and we spend only around 4 percent of our annual budgets on it—a decrease of 500 percent. How did our clothing get so cheap? Well, multinational corporations started making our clothes in places like Vietnam and Bangladesh, where government corruption is rife and officials do little or nothing to stop the victimization of workers. Things like minimum wage, health care, and unions are alien. Workers are likely to work six to seven days a week in a sweltering factory, often in unsafe conditions with little or no protection.[53]

And we're talking about a *lot* of people here. One in six people in the world work in the garment industry. That's just south of 1.5 billion people. For those who care about feminism, approximately 80 percent of those workers are women. *Fewer than 2 percent of them make a living wage.*

No wonder we call a cheap item a "steal." That's exactly what it is. Theft. And we're no Robin Hood stealing from the ultra-rich CEO that we love to villainize; we're more likely stealing from a single mother in Burma just trying to take care of her family.

It's easy to post something on Instagram about how there are twenty-eight million slaves in the world today and we need to #endit. That's great; I'm all for it, genuinely. But many of the clothes we're wearing for our selfie (that we took on a device made in rural China) are *causing* it, not ending it.

As much as I want to believe slavery is a thing of the past, what were most African American slaves doing? Farming cotton. For clothes.

3. Never impulse buy.

It's amazing how much money we blow spur of the moment just because we see a new pair of shoes that we "have to have."

Even though we already have ten pairs of shoes.

Even though we don't have an outfit that even goes with them.

Even though they were made unjustly with polyester that will live on FOREVER in a landfill.

Etc., etc.

It's also amazing that when I exercise self-control and *don't* buy an item, often the desire quickly passes.

As a general rule when you see an item you want, just sit on it for a while. The larger the item, the longer you should wait. Think it over. Give your rational mind time to catch up to your irrational flesh. Pray over it. Remember, God isn't against stuff; he made the world for you to enjoy, and it's beautiful. But if a purchase doesn't have his blessing on it, do you really want it in your life?

You'll be shocked at how good it feels to *not* buy something.

4. When you do buy, opt for fewer, better things.

Often, in an attempt to save money, we end up buying a lot of cheaply (and often unjustly) made items instead of living without for a while and then buying a quality item that will last. "Buy it once" is a great motto to live by. If you can't afford the high-end version, consider used. Either way, in the end you'll save money. And if Jesus was right and all our money is actually God's money and we're just his money managers, then that's a good route.

Still, before you go out and buy some high-quality thing, always ask yourself, *Do I actually need this?*

The English designer William Morris offered a good rule of thumb: "Have nothing in your houses that you do not know to be useful, or believe to be beautiful."[54]

Remember, the world is constantly asking, "How do I get

more?" But the apprentice of Jesus is regularly found asking, "How can I live with less?"

5. When you can, share.

The sharing economy has its downsides, but it's great for simple living. Apps like Lyft and car-sharing services like car2go make it easy to get around cities without owning a car. Vacation rental sites like VRBO make it easy to enjoy the beach without owning a beach house. Not to mention life in community. I share all sorts of things with my community. Why buy a power washer? Matt has one.

As one early church father said, "We hold everything in common except our wives."[55]

Too good.

6. Get into the habit of giving things away.

Remember Jesus on the subject of reality: "It is more blessed to give than to receive." It feels good to put on a new T-shirt, for sure, but it's incredibly life giving to help a child climb out of poverty or just help out a friend in a tough stretch.

Want a more blessed life? Give. Generously. Regularly.

When I first got into minimalism, my favorite part was giving away things I didn't need to people who could actually use them.

Since then our family has established a little "blessing fun" in our monthly budget. It's not much, but it's enough to keep an eye out for people with needs and have a heck of a lot of fun playing Secret Santa.

Less shopping means more money to share, which in turn means a more blessed life.

7. Live by a budget.

It's kind of bizarre to even put this on a list, but I'm shocked at how many people don't have a budget.

A budget is far more than a way to stay out of debt, as vital as that is. A budget is to your money what a schedule is to your time. It's a way to make sure that your "treasure" is going to the right place and not getting squandered.

There are all sorts of great resources for doing a budget Jesus' style, but the key is to actually do it.[56] And then, if you're up for it, share your budget with your community or a close friend. Each year Matt (of power-washer fame) and I redo our budgets together. He has mine; I have his. We can speak into each other's spending habits at any time. We also put a rule in place where we have to get approval for any purchase over a thousand dollars.

Ironically, since we implemented that rule, I haven't had to use it.

8. Learn to enjoy things without owning them.

One quirk of our culture is we think we need to own something to enjoy it. We don't. I deeply enjoy the park down the street from my house. And our local library and the books I get from it. And sitting in Heart Coffee on Twelfth, where the price of admission to stellar design in the heart of downtown is two dollars, for which I also get an excellent cup of Guatemala Rosma. I don't own any of these things. But I enjoy them. So can you.

9. Cultivate a deep appreciation for creation.

Speaking of enjoying things that are free, have you been outside recently? Last I checked, oxygen was still free and a state park was within a short drive. Creation—especially places that are yet untouched by civilization—has the potential to wake us up to our Creator in ways that few things ever can. It invokes gratitude and that secular unicorn, wonder. If materialism despiritualizes us, the material world itself has the opposite effect; it respiritualizes our souls.

10. Cultivate a deep appreciation for the simple pleasures.

The older I get, the more I enjoy the simple things—a cup of coffee or tea in the morning, a home-cooked meal with my family, riding my bike to work on a summer day. These experiences usually cost very little, yet they pay huge dividends of happiness.

Every evening stroll, every sunrise, every good conversation with an old friend is a potential portal to the grateful, joyful enjoyment of life in God's world.

This posture of living says less about our income and more about our relationship to time and the kind of attention we give to God and the goodness of his world.

There's a reason that the teacher in *Ecclesiastes,* at the height of his ostentatious wealth, said, "A person can do nothing better than to eat and drink and find satisfaction in their own toil."[57]

It's the little things, ya know?

11. Recognize advertising for what it is—propaganda. Call out the lie.

As my favorite Quaker so provocatively said, "Refuse to be propagandized by the custodians of modern gadgetry."[58]

This one is actually *fun.* One of the few times where sarcasm feels Jesusy to me. I love to turn this into a game with my kids. When we see an ad, we stop and call out the lie.

See that ad for a new Volvo? The model couple driving off into the Norwegian fjord? Ha. Good one. As if buying that car will make us look like models. The *truth* is . . .

Parenting is a lot of fun.

12. Lead a cheerful, happy revolt against the spirit of materialism.

It was said of Saint Francis and his band of followers that they

"led a cheerful, happy revolt against the spirit of materialism."[59] They saw spreading Jesus' message of simplicity as
one and the same with spreading his message of joy. You
don't have to be grouchy about it or all uptight over how
many socks you own. Just smile, relax, and let joy be your
weapon in the fight.

We often hear, "Less, but better."

But what if less *is* better?

This is the message our culture so desperately needs to hear.

I say it's time for a revolution. Who's with me?

Getting started

Here's a good place to start simplifying: your closet. The
odds are, even if you're a dirt-poor college student (the irony
of that statement . . .), you have a closet. And most of us have
way too many clothes.

The first time I went through my closet, I decided to limit my
wardrobe to six outfits per season. One for every day of the
week, with Sunday as a choose-your-own-adventure day. I
literally had an outfit schedule on the inside of my closet door.
If you saw me on Monday, I was wearing my gray sweatshirt
and black jeans.

A year later I did it again. On round two I realized a different
outfit every single day is kind of ridiculous. By then I also was

aware of the injustice of the fashion industry, which made buying new clothes a total pain in the neck.

So I cut it in half and went down to three outfits per season. Now I was wearing my gray sweatshirt on Mon-Wed-Fri. I loved it.

Recently I went down to two for summer. I alternate every other day, and it feels *great*. I love each outfit. They were both ethically made and environmentally sourced. And for the first time I can ever remember, I have extra money in my clothing budget and no need to spend it. Or desire to.

I feel free.

Now, I'm just assuming that most of us have way too much stuff lying around our homes or apartments. I get that's not true for everybody.

The key is to start wherever the growth edge is for you. If that's your closet and twenty pairs of shoes, cool, start there. If it's your '80s G.I. Joe collection, start there. If it's a fetish for coffee mugs, you know what you need to do.

Remember: the question we should be constantly asking as followers of Jesus isn't actually, What would Jesus do? A more helpful question is, What would Jesus do *if he were me*? If he had my gender, my career, my income, my relationship status? If he was born the same year as me? Lived in the same city as me?

What would that look like?

To follow Jesus is to ask that question until our last breath.

The cost of contentment

In closing, let's be fair: simplicity isn't "the answer" to the hurry of our modern world. (No silver bullet, remember?) But it is *an* answer. Even an easy one. Just get rid of the crap you don't need. But it's not a *cheap* answer. Ironically, it will cost you.

As Dallas Willard so astutely pointed out, the cost of discipleship is high, but the cost of non-discipleship is even *higher.*[60]

Yes, it will cost you to follow Jesus and live his way of simplicity. But it will cost you far more *not* to. It will cost you money and time and a life of justice and the gift of a clean conscience and time for prayer and an unrushed soul and, above all, the "life that is truly life."

I've been thinking about Paul's line in Philippians lately:

I can do all things through [Christ] who strengthens me.[61]

I hear people tear that line out of context all the time. They use it for raising money at the church or getting that promotion or beating cancer or raising a family. All good things. But do you know what Paul was writing about in context?

Contentment.

The line right before that is as follows:

I have learned to be content whatever the circumstances. I know what it is to be in need, and I know what it is to have plenty. I have learned the secret of being content in any and every situation, whether well fed or hungry, whether living in plenty or in want.[62]

In context, Paul wasn't writing about overcoming some allegorical Goliath in our lives; he's writing about one of the greatest enemies of the human soul, before and after Edward Bernays: discontentment. That nagging feeling of always wanting *more*. Not just more stuff, but more *life*. The next thing might not be a thing at all; it might be graduation or marriage or children or a better job or retirement or whatever "it" is for you on the horizon.

But there's always something *just* out of reach. We live with what the historian Arthur Schlesinger called an "inextinguishable discontent."[63] It's what the poet of *Ecclesiastes* described as "a chasing after the wind."[64]

Contentment isn't some Buddhist-like negation of all desire; it's living in such a way that your unfulfilled desires no longer curb your happiness. We all live with unfulfilled desires. In this life all our symphonies remain unfinished. But this doesn't mean we can't live happy.

The truth is you can be happy right here, right now, "through Christ who strengthens me," meaning, through investing your resources in ongoing relational connection to Jesus. You can live a rich and satisfying life whether you are rich or poor, single or married, infertile or counting the days until your four kids are out of the house, crushing it at your dream job or at a minimum wage J.O.B. Right now you have everything you need to live a happy, content life; you have access to the Father. To his loving attention.

Who would have thought it's that easy of a yoke?

Slowing

I like rules.

There, I said it.

Why is everybody so down on rules? What did rules ever do to them? Was there a recent imperialistic rule kleptocracy I missed?

Rules make me feel safe. When I know the rules, I breathe easy.

You're thinking, *Oh brother* . . .

Judgers gonna judge, but I'm a high J on the Myers-Briggs. And, well, I like to have a plan. For everything. I literally sit down before my day off and plan it out by the hour.

Mock me all you want, but I normally have a *really* good day off.

I'm old enough and (hopefully) wise enough to know my personality and laugh about it, living in a way that works for me and not judging my antinomian friends who have other personality types or are in other stages of life. That said, I've started to notice that anti-rule people are often anti-schedule people; and anti-schedule people frequently live in a way that is *reactive,* not *proactive.* As more passenger than driver, consumer than creator. Life happens *to* them, more than *through* them.[1]

Again, the truism: we achieve inner peace when our schedules are aligned with our values. To translate to our apprenticeships to Jesus: if our values are life with Jesus and a growing in maturity toward love, joy, and peace, then our schedules and the set of practices that make up our days and weeks, which together essentially constitute our rules of life, are the ways we achieve inner peace.

Before you anti-rule-P-on-the-MBTI-test people cringe and toss this book across the room, think about it: Could a rule of life even be fun?

There's a new idea in the self-help literature called *gamification.* Basically, the idea is to turn your personal growth into little games. A recent bestseller had the subtitle *The Power of Living Gamefully.*[2] I like that. JMC has a new goal: live gamefully.

So, gameful person that I now am, I'm always on the hunt for little games to play—fun, creative, flexible "rules" to slow down the overall pace of my one-click-below-hurried life.

These rules have just been floating around in the back of my head, so I sat down and put them into writing. Hence, this chapter. Some of the rules are deep and profound; most are quirky and odd. Pick and choose. Steal whatever sounds fun; roll your eyes at the rest.

But before we start, you may be thinking, *Wait, how are these spiritual disciplines?* Well, on one level they aren't. And that's okay, possibly even wise. Jesus lived in a village in the first century, not a city in the twenty-first. Jesus didn't drive a car or field text messages, and a late-night run to Taco Bell wasn't an option. What follows are modern practices based on my attempt at following Jesus while living in a city, raising a family, and having a smartphone, Wi-Fi access, etc. Could it be that we need a few new spiritual disciplines to survive the modern world? Counterhabits to wage war against what the futurist David Zach called "hyperliving—skimming along the surface of life"[3]

So while you won't find the following rules on any standard list of the spiritual disciplines, you *will* find more and more teachers of the way talking about it, as a protest against the new normal of hyperliving.

John Ortberg and Richard Foster both labeled this emerging practice the spiritual discipline of "slowing."[4] Ortberg defined it as "cultivating patience by deliberately choosing to place ourselves in positions where we simply have to wait."[5]

The basic idea behind the practice of slowing is this: slow down your body, slow down your life.

We are *embodied* creatures. Whole people. Our minds are the portals to our whole persons, so how we think has all sorts of ramifications for how we experience life with God. But the mind is not the only portal.

This is why, for example, so few Westerners fast anymore. What was once a core practice for the way of Jesus has fallen by the wayside.[6] We can't fathom a practice that comes at life change through our *stomachs.* We're so used to books and podcasts and university lectures and teachings at church that we often forget: We're not just brains on legs. We're whole people. Holistic, integrated, complex, and full of a dizzying amount of energy. So our apprenticeships to Jesus have to be whole-person endeavors. Mind *and* body.

And if we can slow down both—the pace at which we think and the pace at which we move our bodies through the world—maybe we can slow down our *souls* to a pace at which they can "taste and see that the LORD is good."[7] And that life in his world is good too.

That said, here are twenty ideas for slowing down your overall pace of life. Yup, twenty. I warned you, I like rules.

Let's start with something most of us do daily: drive a car. Even if you live in the city like me and walk or ride your bike most days, the odds are, you still drive on a semi-regular basis. I live right downtown, but I still drive two or three times a week. Here are a few ideas to gamify driving into the spiritual discipline of slowing.

1. Drive the speed limit.

This is a revolutionary idea, never before thought of in a book! If the sign indicates twenty-five miles per hour, *drive twenty-five miles per hour!* Not thirty miles per hour. Not thirty-three (what *can* I get away with?).

Note: not *below* the speed limit—that's just annoying. We'll all hate you.

But right on the money.

Sometimes I do silly things like this just to detox my brain from its addiction to dopamine and the instant gratification of a life of speed. In this case, literally.

2. Get into the slow lane.

Just rock it with Grandma in the Oldsmobile. Or the semi hauling Walmart contraband.

Settle in. Feel the wheel, the road. Watch the scenery pass. Use it as a chance to practice *presence*—to God, to the world, to your own soul.

If you think about it, driving is a great time to pray. Some of my best prayer times are on morning car rides. As I said, I normally ride my bike to get around town, but every few weeks I take an early morning ride across the city to therapy. Overall, I hate driving (one of the reasons I love living in a city), but I look forward to my drive all week long because I know it's a great time to enjoy Jesus' company.

3. Come to a full stop at stop signs.

None of this California nonsense.

By the way, next time you try this, notice how *hard* it is. Maybe that's because I'm from California. But maybe it's because I feel like I'm not moving fast enough, or even because *I'm* not enough . . . there's that disordered heart, right under the surface of my hurry.

4. Don't text and drive.

I should not need to say this; it is, well, *illegal* after all. And the cause of thousands of deaths a year. Our hurry is literally killing us.

But there's a reason most of us text and drive even when we know it's illegal and a life-and-death issue. We're so addicted to the dopamine hit that is our phones that we literally can't just sit in our cars and listen to music or the news or pray or talk with our passengers. We *have* to reach for our phones and risk our necks (and those of others) to get our fix.

Remember the 1950s when people would just go "driving"? Okay, I was born in 1980, so I don't actually remember, but you get the idea. Gender-stereotype warning: the man would wear driving gloves, the woman a colorful head scarf. Let's bring it back: driving.

5. Show up ten minutes early for an appointment, sans phone.

What could you do with ten full leisurely minutes? Bring back coffee-table magazines from the late '90s? Chat with a human being waiting beside you? Read a book?

Here's an idea: What if you prayed?

6. Get in the longest checkout line at the grocery store.

Aah, you're all hating on me now! In an efficiency-obsessed culture, why would we do *that*? That's literally wasting time on purpose.

Well, here's why I do it (sometimes, not always): it's a way to slow down my life and deal with the hurry in my soul. It gives me a few minutes to come off the drug of speed. To pray. To take an inventory of my emotional and spiritual vitals. And, when I get up to the cashier, to express the love of the Father toward him or her, simply by saying hello, asking a few questions, and saying thank you. (Rather than my default of paying for my items while texting with work, while podcasting via headphones, all the while treating the poor cashier like an ATM instead of a soul.)

But here's the deeper motivation: it's wise to regularly deny ourselves from getting what we want, whether through a practice as intense as fasting or as minor as picking the longest checkout line. That way when somebody *else* denies us from getting what we want, we don't respond with anger. We're already acclimated. We don't have to get our way to be happy. Naturally, this takes a while for most of us. So start small, at aisle three.

7. Turn your smartphone into a dumbphone.

A number of years ago, Jake Knapp's article "My Year with a Distraction-Free iPhone (and How to Start Your Own Experiment)" hit the internet like wildfire, and a lot of us joined the movement.[8]

Okay, there's no movement. Just my friend Josh and me. But we're into it.

Since then the catchphrase has become the "dumbphone." As in, well, you get it.

There's no official checklist, but here's what we suggest:

- Take email off your phone.

- Take all social media off your phone, transfer it to a desktop, and schedule set times to check it each day or, ideally, each week.

- Disable your web browser. I'm a bit lenient on this one since I hate surfing the web on my phone and use this only when people send me links. But this is typically a key facet of a dumbphone.

- Delete all notifications, including those for texts. I set my phone so I have to (1) unlock it and (2) click on the text message box to (3) even see if I have any text messages. This was a game changer.

- Ditch news apps or at least news alerts. They are the devil.

- Delete every single app you don't need or that doesn't make your life seriously easier. And keep all the wonder apps that do make life so much easier—maps, calculator, Alaska Airlines, etc. What Knapp put in one box and labeled "The Future."

- Consolidate said apps into a few simple boxes so your home screen is free and clear.

- Finally, set your phone to grayscale mode. This does something neurobiologically that I'm not smart enough to explain, something to do with decreasing dopamine addiction. Google it.

If right now you're thinking, *Why don't you just get a flip phone?* Point taken. So . . .

8. Get a flip phone. Or ditch your cell phone all together.

For post-hipsters with money, get the Punkt phone or the Light Phone II. For the rest of us, trek to your local T-Mobile, which surprisingly has options with no fruit on the back.

9. Parent your phone; put it to bed before you and make it sleep in.

T's and my phones "go to bed" at the same time as our kids: 8:30 p.m., sharp. We literally set them to airplane mode and put them in a drawer in the kitchen. Otherwise we burn time and end up frying our brains with blue screens rather than winding down for bed with a good book or, you know, couples stuff.

10. Keep your phone off until after your morning quiet time.

The stats are ominous: 75 percent of people sleep next to their phones, and 90 percent of us check our phones immediately upon waking.[9]

I can't think of a *worse* way to start my day than a text from my work, a glance at email, a quick (sure . . .) scroll through social media, and a news alert about that day's outrage.

That is a surefire recipe for anger, not love. Misery, not joy. And definitely not peace.

Listen: do not let your phone set your emotional equilibrium and your news feed set your view of the world.

At the risk of coming off angsty and political, remember, "freedom of the press" is a myth. Yes, the press is free from Washington, DC's oversight, which I'm all for. But they are still in slavery to the bottom line. Journalism is a for-profit business—this is capitalism, friends, no matter how far left the journalist may sound. And the reality is, for reasons both neurobiological and theological, *bad news sells.* And click-baity bad news that has something to do with a celebrity (in other words, meaningless trivia) sells even better.

As a result, our morning news feed is *not* an accurate picture of the world. It is curated, not only with a sociopolitical agenda that is thoroughly secular (on both the left and the right) but also with an eye to all that is evil in the world, rarely to *any* of what is good. Because bad news is where the money is.

Don't misread me here; I'm not saying you should close your eyes to injustice in the world. Da-de-dah-de-dah, I can't hear you!

What I'm saying is, let *prayer* set your emotional equilibrium and *Scripture* set your view of the world. Begin your day in the spirit of God's presence and the truth of his Scriptures.

My friends at Red Church in Melbourne, Australia, have this saying: "Win the day." They mean, at the beginning of each day, put your phone on the other side of your house and don't look at it until after you've spent time in devotion to God.

I highly recommend you adopt this practice. This, again, was a game changer for me. A way to keep my priorities in check. More than that, to start my day sitting in love and joy and peace, not getting sucked into the hurry, anxiety, and outrage of the world.

Again, none of this is legalistic. These ideas are simply self-imposed guardrails to keep the trajectory of my life between the lines and on the path (read: way) to life.

11. Set times for email.

This isn't only my suggestion; pretty much every self-help writer, time-management guru, workplace-efficiency expert, opinion blogger, etc. all say the same thing.

Do *not* have email on your phone.

Do *not* glance at it when you get a free moment in the elevator or in a boring meeting.

Do *not* answer random emails throughout the day.

Instead: set a time to do email and stick to it.

I have the luxury of doing email only once a week. Every Monday morning at ten o'clock, I open my inbox and don't stop until I'm down to zero. For the rest of the week, I have an auto reply that basically says, I'll get back to you on Monday.

There are some cons to this approach, but for me the pros far outweigh them.

For most people this is wildly unrealistic—I get it. Figure out what works for you. Most experts recommend you don't check email more than twice a day, say nine o'clock and four o'clock—at the beginning and near the end of your workday. Each time, take your inbox to zero if you can. If there's a task, don't leave it hanging in your email chain; get it onto a to-do list for later.

Unless you're an executive assistant or in some kind of job that requires constant email vigilance, this will save you hours each week. Remember: the more email you do, *the more email you do.* Email pings off itself. That's why when you get back from a long vacation and you're expecting to spend three days going through email, it usually takes just a few hours. Most of it got worked out—shockingly!—without you.

And wow does that feel good.

12. Set a time and a time limit for social media (or just get off it).

In the same vein social media is a black hole. As a tool it's fine. But it's rarely just a tool.

I "have" to be on social media for my work. (Okay, I don't actually have to be on it, but I love writing. And like many people in the knowledge economy, I have to market my work; hence, I'm on Twitter, which, *shh,* secret: I hate. Not exactly the best place for nuance, in-depth thought, and civility.) So I do the same thing as email—once a week. It's not on my phone, so I log on with my laptop at the office, answer every tweet—I'm notorious for the week-late reply—and then set up my posts for the week ahead. All two of them.

And I *loathe* Facebook; it's like the dregs of conservative Christianity. Sorry, I said it. You can post something horrible about me on your page to prove my point.

I enjoy Instagram because I can follow my friends and it's visual. But I don't let myself look at it more than once a day.

Otherwise it just eats up my time and, with it, my joy. Thankfully, there are great apps now to cut you off once you've reached your daily time allowance.

Clearly I'm not a fun follow on social media, but I'm just fine with that. I'm much more interested in standing up on Sunday and having a lot more than 280 characters' worth of things to say. So I'll give my time to that.

13. Kill your TV.

Anybody remember that bumper sticker? Or did I just hopelessly date myself?

Let you in on a secret: I had that one on my car. The Volkswagen. I know, cliché.

But unlike the rest of my former indie-rock friends, I'm nearing the start of my fifth decade and have never bought a TV. Of course, in the day and age of online streaming and devices, that means less than it used to.

Even more than social media, TV (and its sibling, film) consumes the lion's share of our so-called free time. For the average American, that is over five hours a day, or thirty-five hours a week. (Note: it's lower for millennials, but that's only because we spend so much time on social media. We're more addicted to entertainment, not less.)[10]

It's the one addiction for which binging is still socially acceptable. People now have "Netflix days," where they blow an entire day (or weekend) on multiple seasons of the latest streaming phenomenon. It's like Sabbath gone horribly wrong.

Netflix reports that its average user watches a series in *five days,* with millions binging twelve-hour seasons in *a day.*[11]

When asked about the competition from Amazon Prime and other up-and-coming streaming services, Reed Hastings, the CEO of Netflix, shrugged. He said their biggest competition is *sleep.*[12]

And lest you think my crusade is just against time wasted, remember, what we give our attention to is the person we become, for good or evil. As my parents used to tell me, "Garbage in, garbage out." Every . . . single . . . thing that we let into our minds will have an *effect* on our souls.

If you fill your mind with fornication and wildly unrealistic portrayals of beauty, or romance and sex, or violence and the quest for revenge, or cynical secular sarcasm that we call "humor," or a parade of opulent wealth, or simple banality, what shape do you think that will give to your soul?

Honestly, there's very little I *can* watch as an apprentice of Jesus. Central to Jesus' vision of human flourishing is a lust-free life (see Matthew 5v27–30, the Sermon on the Mount). I'm all for art, and even entertainment. But there's very little cinema I can watch that does not incite lust, along with a parade of its ruinous friends. Since the 1920s Hollywood has been at the vanguard of the enemy's quest to degrade sexuality and marriage and desensitize our society to sin. Why make it easy for him?

Occasionally I walk away from a film or show with a sense of wonder, awe, sobriety, or even wisdom. But those inspiring moments are rare.

Why not just get off the crazy train? Kill your TV. I mean, if you want, literally kill it. My friend threw his out the window. Just an idea.

Or here's a more palatable one: set a limit on your entertainment intake. You decide on your number. Two hours a week? Four? Ten? Just set it well below the standard thirty-five.

Our time is our life, and our attention is the doorway to our hearts.

14. Single-task.

One of the reasons I'm so pharisaical about my phone, email, and social media is because I've come to realize the obvious: *multitasking is a myth.* Literally. Only God is omnipresent. I inhabit a body. A body that can do only one . . . thing . . . at . . . a . . . time. Multitasking is just sleight of hand for switching back and forth between a lot of different tasks so I can do them all poorly instead of doing one well.

In the words of a *much* brighter mind, the philosopher Byung-Chul Han:

> The attitude toward time and environment known as "multitasking" does not represent civilizational progress. . . .
> Rather, such an aptitude amounts to regression.

Multitasking is commonplace among wild animals. It is an attentive technique indispensable for survival in the wilderness. . . .

In the wild, the animal is forced to divide its attention between various activities. That is why animals are incapable of contemplative immersion. . . .

Not just multitasking but also activities such as video games produce a broad but flat mode of attention, which is similar to the vigilance of a wild animal. . . . Concern for the good life . . . is yielding more and more to the simple concern for survival.[13]

Or this from the legendary Walter Brueggemann:

Multitasking is the drive to be more than we are, to control more than we do, to extend our power and our effectiveness. Such practice yields a divided self, with full attention given to nothing.[14]

Apparently, I'm not the only one bringing back single-tasking.

No more writing an email while tweeting and fielding text messages on iMessage and listening to music, all while in an open-plan office chatting it up with Sarah in the cubicle next door.

(How's that going for you, anyway?)

I want to be *fully present* to the moment: to God, other people, work in the world, and my own soul. That's more than enough to consume my attention.

I can check the weather and google *Star Wars: Episode X* later.

15. Walk slower.

Okay, some more family-of-origin emo stuff: my dad is type A, like me. When I was a kid, we prided ourselves on how fast we walked. Weird, but true. I remember Christmas shopping with my dad at the mall and just flying past the rest of the shoppers—*suckers!* We're gonna beat them all to J. C. Penney.

My wife is Latina, from a warm culture. She walks slowly. Actually, she does most things slowly. I cannot tell you how many tiffs we got into as a newly married couple over the speed of our walking! Not making this up: *a lot.*

Fast-forward (wait, "walk" forward?) to today and my slow-life revolution: I've noticed that a lot of the greatest followers of Jesus I know—mentors, spiritual directors, older and wiser Jesusy folk—pretty much all walk slow. And it's not because they are dull or out of shape or have asthma. It's on purpose. Deliberate. The by-product of years of apprenticeship under the easy yoke.

Not long ago I was in San Francisco with this older guy who is following Jesus in some really cool ways. We decided to take a stroll rather than sit for coffee. We had a few hours scheduled just to talk and with nowhere to be, but I found myself getting annoyed with his pace. It barely qualified as walking. He moseyed. Any time he had something extra deep to say, he'd fully stop, turn to me, and say it slooowly.

I found myself tapping my feet and feeling all agitated: *Come on, hurry up.*

Then I realized, *Where in the world am I trying to get to so fast? We literally have no place to be!*

Aah . . .

My point is, one of the best ways to slow down your overall pace of life is to *literally* slow down your body. Force yourself to move through the world at a relaxed pace.

All the New Yorkers are hating on me right now. In their defense they *do* have somewhere to be.

Recently T and I were out for a walk, and we got in a little tiff. Nothing heavy, just a minor skirmish.

She was walking too fast . . .

16. Take a regular day alone for silence and solitude.

I take a full day once a month to be alone. Again, not legalistic; sometimes I miss. But usually I wake up early. If the weather is good, I head out to Sauvie Island, a forty-minute drive up the river. In winter I'll book a room at a local Trappist abbey. Just me and the monks.

It's a slow, easy day, full of reading and praying and, yes, occasional napping.

It's Sabbathy but a bit different; it's my time to center. Check my pulse. See if I'm actually living the way I want to live, in line with my convictions. I look back over the previous month; check the schedule for the month ahead. Pull out my life plan and annual goals; track my progress. Journal the ways I sense God coming to me with his invitations.

I absolutely cannot express how much the practice of a monthly day of silence and solitude is formative for my person.

Yes, I'm an introvert; I get most people aren't.

Yes, I'm a pastor; I have semi-flexible hours—I get that.

But I think it's wise for all personality types and far more doable that most people realize.

I wish more people did this. I wish young moms did this while dads watched the kids for one Saturday a month (and vice versa). I wish college kids did this to keep from getting sucked into the insanity of university life where mental illness is at epidemic levels. I wish businesspeople did this to make sure the balance sheet of their lives looked even better than the one at their company. I wish creative, spontaneous, high P on Myers-Briggs, anti-schedule people did this to keep their beautiful, precious, short lives from wasting years on ephemeral distractions.

I wish you did this.

You can.

17. Take up journaling.

I don't journal a lot, just enough to keep focused and justify a Moleskine on my desk. Bare minimum, at my monthly silence and solitude day, I write up any key developments from that month, any dreams, prophetic words, or senses of direction from the Holy Spirit.

This slow, cathartic act of writing your life down is grounding, a tether for the soul in the hurricane of the modern world.

If you don't like to write, keep a vlog or voice note journal. Or just sit and process your life with God. The point is to slow down long enough to observe your life from the outside.

As the Greek once said, "The unexamined life is not worth living."[15]

18. Experiment with mindfulness and meditation.

Again, mindfulness is just silence and solitude for a secular society. It's like prayer, minus the best part.

And there are forms of Jesus mindfulness from the contemplative tradition.[16] On days when I can't focus and my imagination is running naked all over the place (which, unfortunately, is common for me), I take a few minutes and just focus on my breathing. Very basic. I "watch" my breath go in and out.

Then I start to imagine myself breathing in the Holy Spirit and breathing out all the agitation of the day. I turn my breathing into a prayer, inhaling the fruit of the Spirit, one at a time . . .

Breathe in love, breathe out the anger . . .

Breathe in joy, breathe out the sadness and pain . . .

Breathe in peace, breathe out the anxiety and uncertainty of tomorrow . . .

Breathe in patience, breathe out the hurry of my life . . .

Even better than practicing mindfulness is the next step into meditation, another ancient Christian word that's been co-opted by the New Age renaissance. But don't think namaste; think Psalm 1: "Blessed is the one . . . who meditates on his law day and night." In meditation of the Hebrew/Jesus variety, you don't just empty your mind (of the noise, chaos, anxiety, etc.), but you *fill* your mind with Scripture, with truth, with the voice of the Holy Spirit.

I can't put into words what meditation does for my soul. Tim Keller, however, can:

> Persons who meditate become people of substance who have thought things out and have deep convictions, who can explain difficult concepts in simple language, and who have good reasons behind everything they do. Many people do not meditate. They skim everything, picking and choosing on impulse, having no thought-out reasons for their behavior. Following whims, they live shallow lives.[17]

In a cultural moment of shallow, mindfulness and meditation are a step toward the deep waters.

19. If you can, take long vacations.

I've noticed a lot of people don't take long vacations anymore. More like weekend getaways. Head down to LA for a few days. Go to the beach for a weekend. Road-trip to a concert.

This can be a great form of play and a break from routine, which is good and necessary, but often we return home even more tired than before our break. In my experience it takes quite a while to actually slow down long enough to reach a deep place of soul rest.

A recent study documented that only 14 percent of Americans take vacations that last longer than two weeks, and a whopping 37 percent of us take fewer than seven vacation days a year.[18] As the vacations of the middle class become busier and more activity based, coming back from our too-short vacations exhausted is becoming the new normal.

So, most years I save a few vacation days for random things—a wedding, anniversary getaway, that house project. But I take most of it in one long break. People think I'm crazy. Where *were* you? I think I'm onto something.

But this could be just my job rhythms and the need for a break from teaching. A recent study from Finland's University of Tampere found that happiness levels peak on day eight of vacation and then hit a plateau.[19] The researchers recommended we take off one week every quarter (for those with the luxury of four weeks paid vacation time).

Under the Torah, Israel had three feasts a year set aside as a weeklong Sabbath. Zero work allowed, just an extended Sabbath of rest and worship. Usually, the weeklong festival was actually eight days, due to a Sabbath on the front or back end. Ancient wisdom now "proved" by modern science?

I fully get that for many of you this isn't an option, especially for those suffering under the weight of poverty or injustice or just starting out in your career. My encouragement is simply that you take *as long* a vacation as you can, *as often* as you can. Our staff has a rule of life that we sign as part of our employment contracts; on it we literally commit to take all our vacation days each year. I'd encourage you to consider the same.

Summer vacation is one of the most important spiritual disciplines in my life. Yes, that *is* a spiritual discipline. Jesus and most of the great spiritual masters of the Bible regularly went away for weeks at a time, into the eremos. My eremos just has three little kids running around and a stack of novels.

I vote we turn *summer* into a verb again.

20. Cook your own food. And eat in.

We eat in a lot. Tammy and I have a weekly date night, but we rarely eat out as a family. I pack a lunch for work, and our kids just stare at the school cafeteria pizza with existential longing. Most nights we're home. We eat a plant-based, whole-food diet, which means we have to cook a lot of it from scratch. We cook a lot of the same meals to keep things easy. Simplicity in all things.

Fast food is fast, not food. Real food takes time. We're okay with that.

The anchor point for our family's life is the table. We tell stories from the day, highs, lows. Tammy and I ask questions to keep the conversation from devolving into grade-school humor. Welcome neighbors and community. Teach manners as a form of love for neighbor.

After dinner I usually read a chapter from the Bible as we sit around the table. Or just a "proverb of the day."

Recently, we started a new tradition where I introduce a vocabulary word. Each kid tries to use it correctly in a sentence, and the ones who do get a chocolate chip (I'm feeling so much judgment right now . . .).

This, last night, from Jude:

The thing about most homework is, it's *perfunctory.*

But Moses, our eight-year-old, budding creative, has another tack: he makes up a story. Usually it's long, complex, bizarre, and hilarious, and he doesn't use the vocab word until the *last* sentence. By the end of his drama, the other four of us are usually dying with laughter.

Who does that?

Moses, that's who.

These are the moments that make a family a *family.* And some of the best of them happen around a table.

The heart

This chapter was so fun to write, but please don't misread the tone. I'm smiling right now, not glaring. None of this is coming from a high-strung, uptight, religious-guilt-trip kind of heart posture. I promise. Every single rule here is life giving for me. Even fun.

These are just ideas. They might not be for you. That's cool. Come up with your own list. But come up with *a* list. Then do it.

There's more to life than an increase in speed. Life is right under our noses, waiting to be enjoyed.

We must ruthlessly eliminate hurry, and that's best done gamefully.

Epilogue:
A quiet life

It's another Sunday night, still late. Just finished teaching, but only three times, not six.

It was a short bike ride home; made it just in time to kiss the kids good night. Ate a light meal with Tam. No kung fu. My mental health is markedly better. I still haven't finished *The West Wing;* it just hasn't been the same since Sam Seaborn left; maybe I'll watch one episode?

Tomorrow I'll be tired, but I'll still feel my soul.

I'm eating lunch with John again in Menlo Park; we've been doing this every few months. When I say "eating lunch," I mean that he's eating lunch and talking; I mostly take notes and listen.

I open with the customary "How are you?"

He answers, "At this point in my life, I'm just trying to not miss the goodness of each day, and bring my best self to it."

Yes, he says that.

I write it down, verbatim. Grapple with the implications.

Back home on the Sabbath, thinking over my journey. I regret all the years I gave to hurry. And yet. My gratitude for a new kind of life far outweighs any ruefulness over the past.

I guess you could say I feel, well, happy. Not the bright, shiny happy of Instagram or a romantic comedy; that's a chasing after the wind. Like most people, I experience that in occasional bursts, usually on the Sabbath or a special occasion. The rarity of those euphoric moments makes them all the more special.

I resonate deeply with the Alcoholics Anonymous prayer:

> That I may be reasonably happy in this life, and
> supremely happy with [Jesus] forever in the next.[1]

I'm reasonably happy.

Reasonably happy is more than enough.

It's been five years since I quit my job, got off the hurry-train, and opted for the unpaved road into the unknown. People say, "Feels like it was yesterday." But it doesn't feel like yesterday; it feels like another time, another life. One I have zero desire to ever go back to.

The last five years have been healing, disorienting, emotional, fun, difficult, long, full of both joy and disappointment, but mostly just *good*.

I've reorganized my life around three very simple goals:

1. Slow down.

2. Simplify my life around the practices of Jesus.

3. Live from a center of abiding.

Abiding is the metaphor I keep coming back to. I want so badly to live from a deep place of love, joy, and peace.

Nicholas Herman, the Parisian monk better known as Brother Lawrence, called this way of life "the practice of the presence of God"[2] because it takes *practice* to live from attention and awareness. Especially in the modern world.

These four practices—silence and solitude, Sabbath, simplicity, and slowing—have helped me tremendously to move toward abiding as my baseline. But to say it yet *again,* all four of them are a means to an end.

The end isn't silence and solitude; it's to come back to God and our true selves.

It isn't Sabbath; it's a restful, grateful life of ease, appreciation, wonder, and worship.

It isn't simplicity: it's freedom and focus on what matters most.

It isn't even slowing; it's to be *present,* to God, to people, to the moment.

And the goal is practice, not perfection. Multiple times a day, I slip back into hurry. The gravitational pull is overwhelming at times.

Lately, when that happens, I have this little mantra I repeat:

> *Slow down.*
>
> *Breathe.*
>
> *Come back to the moment.*
>
> *Receive the good as gift.*
>
> *Accept the hard as a pathway to peace.*
>
> *Abide.*

It's my rosary, my invocation, my mental and emotional reset. My way to begin again. Some days I say it once; others I forget entirely. On especially stressful days I find myself whispering it under my breath *all* through the day. But each time I recite my little liturgy, I come back to the moment.

The moment is where you find God, find your soul, find your

life. Life isn't "out there" in the next dopamine hit, the next task, the next experience; it's right here, now. As Frank Laubach, who self-identified as a "modern mystic," so beautifully said, "Every now is an eternity if it is full of God."[3]

A contemporary of his, C. S. Lewis, in his already-quoted work of satire on spirituality, had the older, wiser demon say this of the "Enemy" (Jesus):

> The humans live in time but our Enemy destines them to eternity. He therefore, I believe, wants them to attend chiefly to two things, to eternity itself, and to that point of time which they call the Present. For the Present is the point at which time touches eternity . . . .
>
> He would therefore have them continually concerned either with eternity (which means being concerned with Him) or with the Present . . . or else obeying the present voice of conscience, bearing the present cross, receiving the present grace, giving thanks for the present pleasure.[4]

All the best stuff is in the present, the *now.*

All the great wisdom traditions of history, religious and secular, Eastern and Western, Christian and not, have come together on one point: if there's a formula for a happy life, it's quite simple – inhabit the moment.

Each moment is *full* of goodness. Why are we in such a hurry to rush on to the next one? There's *so* much here to *see,* to enjoy, to gratefully receive, to celebrate, to share.

As the poet William Stafford put it, "What can anyone give you greater than now?"[5]

I hate the popular maxim *carpe diem.* It's Latin, but what could be more American? Seize the day! As if time is a precious commodity and it's every man for himself.

What if the day, what if time itself isn't a scarce resource to seize but a gift to receive with grateful joy?

I'm just trying to not miss the goodness of each day.

Even on the bad days, in the hard moments, in the pain, the crisis, or disappointment, the diagnosis, the grief over all the ways life is less than what it could or should be, even *then,* I think of AA's wonderful line: "Accepting hardship as the pathway to peace; taking, as [Jesus] did, this sinful world as it is, not as I would have it."[6]

Our days of pain are the building blocks of our character. Our crucible of Christlikeness. I rarely welcome them—I'm not that far down the path, not yet—but I accept them. Because my Rabbi teaches that happiness isn't the result of circumstances but of character and communion.[7]

So whether it's a good day or a not-so-good day, either way, I don't want to miss the moment.

If it's true that goodness and mercy follow me "all the days of my life,"[8] how many days do I *miss* that goodness in my helter-skelter race to cram it all in before sunset? Rush past that mercy in my blitzkrieg through urban life? "I'll sleep when

I'm dead" is the mantra of a soul living in denial of God and outside the flow of eternity.

No more. I commit from here on to ruthlessly eliminate hurry.

I fail, naturally.

Multiple times a day.

And when I do? I begin again . . .

> *Slow down.*
>
> *Breathe.*
>
> *Come back to the moment . . .*

I wish I could tell you that after a few years of practice I have this *down.* I'm never in a hurry. Consider it eliminated, check. I just live and love in a perpetual zen-like state of Jesus-derived joy and peace.

Alas, I live in the same place as you: the modern world. With all its privilege and all its pain. All its wealth and hedonic pleasure and good coffee and urban delight, alongside its stress and digital distraction and overconsumption and bone-tiring demands. Hence, this book, which was for me as much as you.

The world hasn't changed one bit in the last five years; if anything, it's gone farther off the rails. But I've changed. I no longer experience the world in the same way. I'm on a new trajectory. And when I look over the horizon at the man I'm becoming, it's obvious I still have a long, long way to go, but I like the line on the horizon. Even now there are moments when I see that future me in the present, where I embody what Edward Friedman called "a non-anxious presence."[9] It feels so, so good. Then I predictably get sucked back into hurry, usually several times a day. I lose my emotional equilibrium. I fall out of sync with the Spirit.

When that happens, I reset. Begin again. This time, slowly . . .

> *Breathe.*
>
> *Come back to the moment.*
>
> *Receive the good as gift.*
>
> *Accept the hard as gift . . .*

As fun as this book was to write, the fact is, there's no silver bullet, no killer app, no unisize formula. Those four practices? They are exactly that, practices. Next steps to move forward on a lifelong journey in which you never "arrive."

But if your journey is anything like mine, it will feel like three steps forward, two steps back. That's normal, healthy even. The key is to keep at it. The tortoise, not the proverbial hare. When you err, just begin again.

A year after I got back from sabbatical, I taught through Paul's letter to the Thessalonians. After three months of sitting in his short missive, one line in particular kept coming back to haunt me. Something about it imprinted on my brain; it's become my manifesto.

Make it your ambition to lead a quiet life.[10]

I'm struck by the juxtaposition of Paul's words.

The word "ambition" next to the word "quiet."

Those two words sound like enemies, not friends. When I hear *ambition,* I generally think of hurry (or its new synonym: "hustle") and all that comes with a driven, careerist kind of life. I imagine the latest celeb entrepreneur or type A professional—driven to succeed, even at the cost of his or her soul.

But Paul says we are to aim our ambition—the pent-up energy and drive that we *all* have at some level—at something else entirely: a quiet life.

That's the goal, the end, the vision of success: a quiet life.

Of all the adjectives on offer, Paul opts for *quiet.*

Not *loud.*

Not *important.*

Not even *impactful.*

Just quiet.

Paul's line reminds me of the long-standing advice of Saint Ignatius of Loyola (founder of the Jesuit order):

Try to keep your soul always in peace and quiet.[11]

I smile every time I read Ignatius; I love that he said "try." As if he knew we'd mess it up, daily. As if he knew how long the journey was from reality to possibility. From who we are to who we have the potential to grow and mature into. From Jesus' invitation of "Come" and take up the easy yoke to Paul's dying eulogy: "The time for my departure is near. I have fought the good fight."[12]

To live a quiet life in a world of noise is a fight, a war of attrition, a calm rebellion against the status quo.

And like any fight, death comes with the territory. As does sacrifice. For me, I had to die to who I could have been if I'd stayed on the path of upward mobility. Even now there are rare moments when I'll think, *What if?*

I had to make peace with who I am. And who I'm *not.*

I had to let go of the envy, the fantasy, the cancerous restlessness.

To accept, gratefully: this is my life.

There's a death in that, true. But in the cruciform kingdom, only the bad things die: image and status and bragging rights, all vanity. More importantly: death is always followed by resurrection.

Aim at an easy life and your actual life will be marked by a gnawing angst and frustration; aim at an easy yoke and, as

John Ortberg once said, "Your capacity for tackling hard assignments will actually grow."[13]

What's hard isn't following Jesus. What's hard is following myself, doing my life my way; therein lies the path to exhaustion. With Jesus there's still a yoke, a weight to life, but it's an easy yoke, and we never carry it alone.

But this easy yoke to carry a hard life is something we have to fight for. *Ugh,* you're thinking. *I don't want a fight; I want a vacation.* But the hard reality is the fight isn't optional. On this, evolutionary biology and Christian theology agree: life is a struggle. The question is simply: What are you fighting *for*? Survival of the fittest? Some perversion of the American dream? Or something better?

Should you enlist in the war on hurry, remember what's at stake. You're not just fighting for a good life but for a good *soul.*

So, dear reader and friend, you, like me, must make a decision. Not just when your own fork-in-the-road kind of midlife crisis comes (and it *will* come), but every day.

How will you live?

In the years to come, our world will most likely go from fast to faster; more hurried, more soulless, more vapid; "deceiving and being deceived."[14] Will you traverse that road? Will you follow the same old, tired, uncreative story of hurry and busyness and noisy, materialistic, propagandized living? Just try to add in a little Jesus as you careen through life? Make it

to church when you can? Pray when you find the time?
Mostly just stay ahead of the wolf pack?

Or . . .

Will you remember there's another road, another way? Will
you off-ramp onto the narrow path? Will you radically alter the
pace of your life to take up the easy yoke of Jesus?

And when you fail, begin again. This time: slowly.

This book is both a question and an answer. But mostly it's
an invitation, from one invitee to another.

"Come to me. . . . Find rest for your souls."

I say yes.

You?

Here's to the easy yoke.

**We urge you,
brothers and sisters
. . . to make it your
ambition to lead
a quiet life.**

**−Paul in
1 Thessalonians
4v10−11**

Thanks

T, I love you.

Jude, Moto, Sunday, can't wait
for Sabbath.

Our "love feast" community
(Normans, Smits, Hooks, Peter-
sons, Mossers, Pam, Hanna).

Comers and Jaureguis—familia!

John Ortberg, for the best lunch I've ever had.

"Chris and Meryl."

Dr. Jim, mind ninja.

Dave Lomas, for Friday calls.

The Searock Fraternity (Dave, Jonny, Pete, Tim, Al, Darren, Todd, Mark, Tyler, Jon, Evan). Love you all deeply. See you in May.

Bridgetown Church and staff, for giving me time to write (and a zillion other things).

G.

Bethany, for being the most encouraging person I know.

R.W.P.

Mike S and the crew at Y&Y.

Everybody from WaterBrook who made this book possible.

My love and gratitude for you all run deep, very deep.

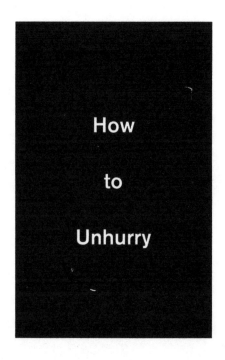

How

to

Unhurry

Ideas are just the beginning. Unless they move from your
mind into your body, they don't become reality.
To that end, I've made a short workbook with some
exercises to get you started on each of the four practices.

It's available at:
johnmarkcomer.com/howtounhurry

Notes

Prologue: Autobiography of an epidemic

1. This was before his come-back as John Wick. Not that I've seen that movie. That would be very unJesusy . . .

2. I like the definition of *mega* as "(1) Sunday centric, (2) personality driven, and (3) consumer-oriented program-ming." You can do church that way with two thousand, two hundred, or twenty.

3. This line is originally from Peter Scazzero in a book that's shaped my life and our church in profound ways: *The Emotionally Healthy Church: A Strategy for Discipleship That Actually Changes Lives* (Grand Rapids, MI: Zondervan, 2003), 20. I'll reference it quite a bit in the pages to come.

4. For you Portlanders, Twenty-Third used to be cool. I'm dating myself, but I remember when Urban Outfitters was brand-new. It was a thing. Trust me.

5. Byung-Chul Han, *The Burnout Society* (Stanford, CA: Stanford University Press, 2015), 51.

6. Gilles Lipovetsky, *Hyper-modern Times* (Malden, MA: Polity Press, 2005).

7. Matthew 11v28–30.

8. Matthew 11v30, MSG.

9. Hebrews 1v9.

Hurry: the great enemy of spiritual life

1. All of John Ortberg's books are great, but *Eternity Is Now in Session: A Radical Rediscovery of What Jesus Really Taught About Salvation, Eternity, and Getting to the Good Place* (Carol Stream, IL: Tyndale, 2018) and *Soul Keeping: Caring for the Most Important Part of You* (Grand Rapids, MI: Zondervan, 2014) are two of my faves.

2. Please put this book down, go buy Dallas Willard's *Renova-tion of the Heart: Putting on the Character of Christ* (Colorado Springs, CO: NavPress, 2002), and read it instead.

3. Which book do I start with, you ask? Oh my, an impossible question. *The Divine Conspir-acy: Rediscovering Our Hidden Life in God* (New York: Harper-Collins, 1998) is Dallas Willard's magnum opus. *The Spirit of the Disciplines: Understanding How God Changes Lives* (New York: HarperCollins, 1988) is the most influential book I've ever read. But those are his two hardest to read. *The Great Omission: Reclaiming Jesus's Essential Teachings on Discipleship* (New York: HarperCollins, 2006) is his easiest read and does a great job of capturing the gist of his life message. And *Renovation of the Heart* is the best all-in-one-place read for Willard's work. Choose your own adventure!

4. I'm paraphrasing his question, based on the title of John Ortberg's excellent book *The Me I Want to Be: Becoming God's Best Version of You* (Grand Rapids, MI: Zondervan, 2014). It's so, so good.

5. This story is also found on page 20 of *Soul Keeping* by John Ortberg, which, by the way, is a gem of a book. I read it every summer. I paraphrased Ortberg's language a bit, but the Willard quote is verbatim.

6. Michael Zigarelli, "Distracted

from God: A Five-Year, World-wide Study," Christianity 9 to 5, 2008, www.christianity9to5.org/distracted-from-god.

7. See Mark 12v28–31, where Jesus quotes two commands, the first from Deuteronomy 6v4–5 and the second from Leviticus 19v18.

8. 1 Corinthians 13v4.

9. Kosuke Koyama, *Three Mile an Hour God* (Maryknoll, NY: Orbis, 1980), 7.

10. *Merriam-Webster Dictionary,* s.v. "slow."

11. Father Walter Adams, quoted in Alan Fadling, *An Hurried Life: Following Jesus' Rhythms of Work and Rest* (Downers Grove, IL: InterVarsity Press, 2013), 94.

12. Ronald Rolheiser, *The Holy Longing: The Search for a Christian Spirituality* (New York: Random House, 2014), 31–33. The next book in that series, *Sacred Fire: A Vision for a Deeper Human and Christian Maturity* (New York: Random House, 2014), is one of my all-time favorite books. It's all about discipleship in your thirties and forties and is a must-read for all thirtysomethings who follow Jesus.

13. T. S. Eliot, "Burnt Norton," *Four Quartets* (New York: Harcourt, 1943).

14. John Ortberg, *The Life You've Always Wanted: Spiritual Disciplines for Ordinary People* (Grand Rapids, MI: Zondervan, 2002), 38–39. I simply love Ortberg's writing. All his books are good, but this is one of his best.

15. Luke 10v41–42.

16. This phrase is from Peter Scazzero's *Emotionally Healthy Spirituality: It's Impossible to Be Spiritually Mature While Remaining Emotionally Immature* (Grand Rapids, MI: HarperCollins, 2017), one of the most important books I've ever read. Can't encourage you enough to read it. I read it every summer without fail.

A brief history of speed

1. *Encyclopaedia Britannica* estimates that the first sundial used by the Romans was set up in 290 BC, with one designed for the city being built in approximately 164 BC; www.britannica.com/technology/sundial.

2. Aulus Gellius, *The Complete Works of Aulus Gellius: Attic Nights* (East Sussex, UK: Delphi Classics, 2016), attributes these lines to the Roman comic playwright Plautus.

3. Carl Honore, *In Praise of Slowness: Challenging the Cult of Speed* (New York: HarperCollins, 2004), 22.

4. Jacques Le Goff, *Time, Work, and Culture in the Middle Ages,* trans. Arthur Goldhammer (Chicago: University of Chicago Press, 1980), 44.

5. Daniel J. Boorstin, *The Discoverers: A History of Man's Search to Know His World and Himself* (New York: Vintage Books, 1983), 39.

6. Arwen Curry, "How Electric Light Changed the Night," KQED, January 20, 2015, www.kqed.org/science/26331/how-electric-light-changed-the-night.

7. Kerby Anderson, *Technology and Social Trends: A Biblical Point of View* (Cambridge, OH: Christian Publishing, 2016), 102.

8. In my defense, one study said Americans work 137 more hours per year than the Japanese, 260 more hours per year than the British, and 499 more hours per year than the French. See Stacy Weckesser, "Americans Are Now Working More Hours Than Any Country in the World," Blue Water Credit, July 21, 2015, https://bluewatercredit.com/americans-now-working-hours-country-world.

9. Lawrence Mishel, "Vast Majority of Wage Earners Are Working Harder, and for Not Much More: Trends in U.S. Work Hours and Wages over 1979–2007," Economy Policy Institute, January 30, 2013, www.epi.org/publication/ib348-trends-us-work-hours-wages-1979-2007.

10. Silvia Bellezza, Neeru Paharia, and Anat Keinan, "Research: Why Americans Are So Impressed by Busyness," *Harvard Business Review,* December 15, 2016, https://hbr.org/2016/12/research-why

-americans-are-so-impressed -by-busyness.

11. Andrew Sullivan, "I Used to Be a Human Being," *New York Times Magazine,* September 19, 2016, http://nymag.com /intelligencer/2016/09/andrew -sullivan-my-distraction-sickness -and-yours.html.

12. For a fascinating read on 2007 and just how much has changed, pick up Thomas L. Friedman, *Thank You for Being Late: An Optimist's Guide to Thriving in the Age of Accelerations* (New York: Farrar, Straus and Giroux, 2016).

13. Nicholas Carr, *The Shallows: What the Internet Is Doing to Our Brains* (New York: W. W. Norton, 2011), 6–7.

14. Julia Naftulin, "Here's How Many Times We Touch Our Phones Every Day," Business Insider, July 13, 2016, www .businessinsider.com/dscout -research-people-touch-cell -phones-2617-times-a-day -2016-7.

15. Kari Paul, "Millennials Waste Five Hours a Day Doing This One Thing," *New York Post,* May 18, 2017, https://nypost.com /2017/05/18/millennials-waste -five-hours-a-day-doing-this-one -thing.

16. Michael Winnick and Robert Zolna, "Putting a Finger on Our Phone Obsession: Mobile Touches: A Study on Humans and Their Tech," *dscout* (blog), June 16, 2016, https://blog .dscout.com/mobile-touches.

17. Robinson Meyer, "Your Smartphone Reduces Your Brainpower, Even If It's Just Sitting There: A Silent, Powered-Off Phone Can Still Distract the Most Dependent Users," *Atlantic,* August 2, 2017, www .theatlantic.com/technology /archive/2017/08/a-sitting -phone-gathers-brain-dross /535476.

18. Visit www.tristanharris.com, or watch his TED talk: "Tristan Harris: Do Our Devices Control More Than We Think?," October 13, 2017, TED Radio Hour, https://wnyc.org/story/tristan -harris-do-our-devices-control -more-than-we-think.

19. Mike Allen, "Sean Parker Unloads on Facebook: 'God

Only Knows What It's Doing to Our Children's Brains,'" Axios, November 9, 2017, www.axios .com/sean-parker-unloads-on -facebook-god-only-knows-what -its-doing-to-our-childrens-brains -1513306792-f855e7b4-4e99 -4d60-8d51-2775559c2671.html.

20. Kevin McSpadden, "You Now Have a Shorter Attention Span Than a Goldfish," *Time,* May 14, 2015, http://time.com /3858309/attention-spans -goldfish.

21. This idea comes from Seth Godin's great blog post "When Your Phone Uses You," *Seth's Blog* (blog), September 30, 2016, https://seths.blog/2016/12 /when-your-phone-uses-you.

22. Listen to "Teach Us to Pray—Week 2" from my friend Jon Tyson of Church of the City New York, www.youtube.com /watch?v=Jb0vxXZuqek. His thesis: "Distraction leads to disillusionment; attention leads to adoration."

23. This quote is from this fantastic article by Paul Lewis: "'Our Minds Can Be Hijacked':

the Tech Insiders Who Fear a Smartphone Dystopia," *Guardian,* October 6, 2017, www .theguardian.com/technology /2017/oct/05/smartphone -addiction-silicon-valley -dystopia.

24. "Continuous Partial Attention: What Is Continuous Partial Attention?," Linda Stone, https:// lindastone.net/qa/continuous -partial-attention.

25. Cory Doctorow, "Writing in the Age of Distraction," *Locus Magazine,* January 7, 2009, www.locusmag.com/Features /2009/01/cory-doctorow-writing -in-age-of.html.

26. Aldous Huxley, *Brave New World Revisited* (New York: HarperCollins, 1958), 35.

27. Tony Schwartz, "Addicted to Distraction," *New York Times,* November 28, 2015, www .nytimes.com/2015/11/29 /opinion/sunday/addicted-to -distraction.html.

28. Neil Postman, *Technopoly: The Surrender of Culture to Technology* (New York: Vintage, 1993), 185.

Something is deeply wrong

1. As far as I can tell, this story was first told in Lettie Cowman's book *Springs in the Valley* (Grand Rapids, MI: Zondervan, 1968), 207. But it's best known from John O'Donohue, *Anam Cara* (New York: HarperCollins, 1997), 151. His quote is "We have moved too quickly to reach here; now we need to wait to give our spirits a chance to catch up with us." Honestly, I'm not sure of the accuracy of this story. But fiction or non, there's truth in it.

2. Rosemary K. M. Sword and Philip Zimbardo, "Hurry Sickness: Is Our Quest to Do All and Be All Costing Us Our Health?," *Psychology Today,* February 9, 2013, www.psychologytoday.com/us/blog/the-time-cure/201302/hurry-sickness.

3. Meyer Friedman and Ray H. Rosenman, *Type A Behavior and Your Heart* (New York: Knopf, 1974), 33.

4. Friedman and Rosenman, *Type A,* 42.

5. Sword and Zimbardo, "Hurry Sickness."

6. This list is my adaptation of Ruth Haley Barton's in *Strengthening the Soul of Your Leadership* (Downers Grove, IL: InterVarsity Press, 2018), 104–6, an excellent book. Here is Barton's list in full: "irritability or hypersensitivity," "restlessness," "compulsive overworking," "emotional numbness," "escapist behaviors," "disconnected from our identity and calling," "not able to attend to human needs," "hoarding energy," and "slippage in our spiritual practices."

7. If it makes you feel better, the first time I took Barton's self-inventory, I scored 9 for 9. As in, check me into the detox center now.

8. "APA Public Opinion Poll: Annual Meeting 2018," American Psychiatric Association, March 23–25, 2018, www.psychiatry.org/newsroom/apa-public-opinion-poll-annual-meeting-2018.

9. Thomas Merton, *Conjectures*

of a Guilty Bystander (New York: Doubleday, 1966), 81, which, by the way, was written over fifty years ago.

10. Wayne Muller, *Sabbath: Finding Rest, Renewal, and Delight in Our Busy Lives* (New York: Bantam, 1999), 2.

11. Mary Oliver, *Upstream: Selected Essays* (New York: Penguin, 2016), from "Section One: Upstream." She said that at the end of an essay about nature, but I think it's true of all relationships—with the earth, people, and most of all God.

12. Matthew 6v21.

13. John Ortberg, *The Life You've Always Wanted: Spiritual Disciplines for Ordinary People* (Grand Rapids, MI: Zondervan, 2002), 79.

14. William Irvine, *A Guide to the Good Life: The Ancient Art of Stoic Joy* (New York: Oxford University Press, 2009), 1–2.

15. Mark 8v36.

Hint: the solution isn't more time

1. My three favorites are Greg McKeown's *Essentialism: The Disciplined Pursuit of Less* (New York: Crown, 2014); Joshua Fields Millburn and Ryan Nicodemus's *Essential: Essays by the Minimalists* (Missoula, MT: Asymmetrical Press, 2015); and Cal Newport's *Deep Work: Rules for Focused Success in a Distracted World* (New York: Grand Central, 2016). FYI.

2. Genesis 1v27.

3. Genesis 2v7.

4. As great as they are—love you all! That said, there is another book I adore, *The Emotionally Healthy Church: A Strategy for Discipleship That Actually Changes Lives* (Grand Rapids, MI: Zondervan, 2003) by Peter Scazzero. He has a chapter on exactly that: accepting your limitations.

5. Genesis 3v5.

6. 1 Corinthians 13v9.

7. Hosea 4v6.

8. James 4v14, MSG.

9. John 21v22.

10. He said this in his podcast, *The Emotionally Healthy Leader,* which is one podcast I never miss an episode of. Peter

Scazzero, "Six Marks of a Church Culture That Deeply Changes Lives: Part 1," March 5, 2019, www.emotionallyhealthy.org /podcast/detail/Six-Marks-of-a -Church-Culture-that-Deeply -Changes-Lives:-Part-1.

11. Matthew 5v3.

12. Matthew 5–7.

13. Anne Lamott, *Operating Instructions: A Journal of My Son's First Year* (New York: Anchor, 2005), 84–85.

14. Henry David Thoreau, *Walden* (Edinburgh, UK: Black & White Classics, 2014), 51. The first few chapters are *gold,* and then it's endless pontificating about trees. I'm all for trees, but . . .

15. Philip Zimbardo, *The Demise of Guys: Why Boys Are Struggling and What We Can Do About It* (self-pub, Amazon Digital Services, 2012). Or read this simple summary of his research at Ashley Lutz, "Porn and Video Games Are Ruining the Next Generation of American Men," Business Insider, June 1, 2012, www .businessinsider.com/the -demise-of-guys-by-philip -zimbardo-2012-5.

16. This quote and the previous stats are from Charles Chu's excellent article on Medium, "The Simple Truth Behind Reading 200 Books a Year," January 6, 2017, https:// medium.com/s/story/the -simple-truth-behind-reading -200-books-a-year-1767cb03 af20. Fun fact: if the average person spent his or her annual 3,442.5 hours of social media and TV on reading instead, he or she'd come in at more than 1,600 books per year. Just saying.

17. Ephesians 5v15–16, ESV.

18. These translations are from the KJV, NIV, and MSG respectively.

The secret of the easy yoke

1. John 10v10.

2. Romans 1v16.

3. Matthew 4v19.

4. Matthew 11v28–30.

5. Anne Helen Petersen, "How Millennials Became the Burnout

Generation," BuzzFeed, January 5, 2019, www.buzzfeednews .com/article/annehelenpetersen? /millennials-burnout-generation -debt-work.

6. Dallas Willard, *The Spirit of the Disciplines: Understanding How God Changes Lives* (New York: HarperCollins, 1988), 5. This is a gem of a book. I read it regularly.

7. Eugene H. Peterson, *The Jesus Way: A Conversation on the Ways That Jesus Is the Way* (Grand Rapids, MI: Eerdmans, 2007), 4. The opening chapter alone is worth the price of admission.

8. Frederick Dale Bruner, *Matthew: A Commentary, Volume 1: The Christbook, Matthew 1–12* (Grand Rapids, MI: Eerdmans, 2004), 538. Bruner's commentary is a masterpiece.

9. Full disclosure: this line is a blatant steal from *Soul Keeping: Caring for the Most Important Part of You* (Grand Rapids, MI: Zondervan, 2014), by John Ortberg, which is kind of like this book but better!

What we're really talking about is a rule of life

1. John 11v6–7.

2. Mark 5v23, ESV.

3. Mark 5v24–34.

4. Richard A. Swenson, *Margin: Restoring Emotional, Physical, Financial, and Time Reserves to Overloaded Lives* (Colorado Springs: NavPress, 2004), 69.

5. Matthew 11v30, MSG.

6. John 15v1–8, ESV.

7. Matthew 6v33, ESV.

Intermission: Wait, what are the spiritual disciplines again?

1. That, and a few things the Reformation got wrong, such as *grace* being antithetical to any kind of self-effort, *law* and *works* referring to self-effort in general and not more specifi- cally to the Jewish Torah, and the redefinition of *good works* to mean, really, "bad works." The Reformers got a lot right, and for that I'm deeply grateful. However, they never finished.

But that is a whole other book.

2. Matthew 5v19; 7v24.

3. 1 Corinthians 9v24–27.

4. This is from Dallas Willard, *The Spirit of the Disciplines: Understanding How God Changes Lives* (New York: HarperCollins, 1988), 68, hands down the best book I've found on the subject.

Silence and solitude

1. Kevin McSpadden, "You Now Have a Shorter Attention Span Than a Goldfish," *Time,* May 14, 2015, http://time.com /3858309/attention-spans -goldfish.

2. Andrew Sullivan, "I Used to Be a Human Being," *New York Times Magazine,* September 19, 2016, http://nymag.com /intelligencer/2016/09/andrew -sullivan-my-distraction-sickness -and-yours.html.

3. Ronald Rolheiser, *The Holy Longing: The Search for a Christian Spirituality* (New York: Random House, 2014), 32.

4. Matthew 3v17.

5. Matthew 4v1–3.

6. Mark 1v35.

7. Mark 1v36–37.

8. Okay, so I'm not Eugene Peterson.

9. Mark 1v38.

10. Mark 6v31.

11. Mark 6v31.

12. Mark 6v32.

13. Mark 6v33–35.

14. Mark 6v45–47.

15. Luke 5v15–16.

16. See his poem "Entering into Joy."

17. Saint John Climacus, *The Ladder of Divine Ascent* (London: Faber & Faber, 1959), 135.

18. Here's the full quote from *The Screwtape Letters* by C. S. Lewis (remember, this is a demon writing, so everything is flipped): "Music and silence— how I detest them both! How thankful we should be that ever since Our Father entered Hell—though longer ago than humans, reckoning in light years, could express—no square inch of infernal space and no moment of infernal time has been surrendered to either of those abominable forces, but all has been occupied by Noise—Noise, the grand dynamism, the audible expression of all that is exultant, ruthless, and virile—Noise which alone defends us from silly qualms, despairing scruples and impossible desires. We will make the whole universe a noise in the end. We have already made great strides in this direction as regards the Earth. The melodies and silences of Heaven will be shouted down in the end. But I admit we are not yet loud enough, or anything like it. Research is in progress."

19. Richard J. Foster, *Celebration of Discipline: The Path to Spiritual Growth* (New York: HarperCollins, 1998), 96.

20. The major exception to this is what Saint John of the Cross and others call the "dark night of the soul." This is where we practice all the spiritual disciplines, but for a season we don't feel God's presence. If you're in that kind of a dark night, then read Saint John's book *Dark Night of the Soul.* Or read *The Dark Night of the Soul: A Psychiatrist Explores the Connection Between Darkness and Spiritual Growth* (New York: HarperCollins, 2004), Gerald May's book on Saint John's book, which in my own dark night I found even more helpful.

21. Henri Nouwen, *Making All Things New: An Invitation to the Spiritual Life* (New York: HarperCollins, 1981), 69, 71. His honest work on silence and solitude, its promise and its difficulty, is superb.

22. Henri Nouwen, *Spiritual Direction: Wisdom for the Long Walk of Faith* (New York: HarperOne, 2006), 5.

23. Mark 6v31, ESV.

24. John 8v31, ESV.

25. A beautiful line from Thomas R. Kelly's masterpiece *A Testament of Devotion* (New York: HarperCollins, 1992), 100.

26. Sullivan, "I Used to Be a Human Being."

Sabbath

1. Ecclesiastes 1v8, ESV.

2. That would be our friend

Mick Jagger singing for the Rolling Stones, "(I Can't Get No) Satisfaction," 1965.

3. Karl Rahner, *Servants of the Lord* (New York: Herder and Herder, 1968), 152.

4. Saint Augustine of Hippo, *The Confessions of Saint Augustine* (New York: Doubleday, 1960), 43.

5. Dallas Willard, *Life Without Lack: Living in the Fullness of Psalm 23* (Nashville: Nelson, 2018). This is his newest book (published after his death) from a series of lectures he gave at his church. It's far easier to read than his other books. I read it three times last year. It's that good.

6. Wayne Muller, *Sabbath: Restoring the Sacred Rhythm of Rest* (New York: Bantam, 1999), 10.

7. Hebrews 4v11.

8. Walter Brueggemann, *Sabbath as Resistance: Saying No to the Culture of Now* (Louisville, KY: Westminster John Knox Press, 2014), 107.

9. Mark 2v27.

10. Unless you grew up as a Seventh-day Adventist or in one of the few Western denominations that has a value for Sabbath.

11. A. J. Swoboda, *Subversive Sabbath: The Surprising Power of Rest in a Nonstop World* (Grand Rapids, MI: Brazos, 2018), 5; this is my favorite book of A. J.'s and one of my favorite books on the Sabbath.

12. For those of you freaking out right now over "six days," here are two book recommendations: John H. Walton, *The Lost World of Genesis One: Ancient Cosmology and the Origins Debate* (Downers Grove, IL: InterVarsity, 2009); and John H. Sailhamer, *Genesis Unbound: A Provocative New Look at the Creation Account* (Colorado Springs: Dawson Media, 1996). My two faves on the debate.

13. Genesis 2v2–3.

14. Swoboda, *Subversive Sabbath,* 11.

15. Bob Sullivan, "Memo to Work Martyrs: Long Hours Make You Less Productive," CNBC, January 26, 2015, www.cnbc.com/2015/01/26/working

-more-than-50-hours-makes
-you-less-productive.html.

16. Dan Allender, *Sabbath* (Nashville: Thomas Nelson, 2009), 4–5.

17. Genesis 1v22, ESV.

18. Genesis 1v28, ESV.

19. Ryan Buxton, "What Seventh-Day Adventists Get Right That Lengthens Their Life Expectancy," *HuffPost,* July 31, 2014, www.huffingtonpost. com/2014/07/31/seventh-day -adventists-life-expectancy_n _5638098.html.

20. Another fun tidbit: one legend says the pioneers who Sabbathed on the Oregon Trail arrived there before those who didn't.

21. Exodus 19v6.

22. Exodus 20v8.

23. Exodus 20v9–10.

24. Eugene H. Peterson, *The Pastor: A Memoir* (New York: HarperOne, 2011), 220; my favorite of all his books.

25. Exodus 20v11. I actually skipped the middle part; the verbatim command is even longer.

26. This is from Deuteronomy 5v12–14. Most of the material after this was inspired by Walter Brueggemann, *Sabbath as Resistance,* which is absolutely phenomenal.

27. Deuteronomy 5v15.

28. Exodus 1v11.

29. Alexander Harris, "U.S. Self-Storage Industry Statistics," SpareFoot, December 19, 2018, https://sparefoot.com/self -storage/news/1432-self-storage -industry-statistics. These stats are from 2018 and are projected to rise.

30. Jon McCallem, "The Self-Storage Self," *New York Times Magazine,* September 2, 2009, https://nytimes.com /2009/09/06/magazine/06self -storage-t.html.

31. That's the number thrown around, but it's wildly debated, as it's tricky to track. Here's a legit study that actually puts it much higher at forty million: "Global Estimates of Modern Slavery," International Labour Organization and Walk Free Foundation, 2017, 5, www.ilo .org/wcmsp5/groups/public /@dgreports/@dcomm

/documents/publication/wcms
_575479.pdf.

32. "Global Wealth Pyramid: Decreased Base," Credit Suisse Research Institute, December 1, 2018, www.credit-suisse.com /corporate/en/articles/news -and-expertise/global-wealth -pyramid-decreased-base -201801.html.

33. Brueggemann, *Sabbath as Resistance,* 101. Super fun little read.

34. Psalm 23v1.

35. Ronald Rolheiser, *Forgotten Among the Lilies: Learning to Love Beyond Our Fears* (New York: Doubleday, 2004), 16.

36. Confession: I fudged this. Restlessness is a major theme in Rolheiser's writings. This second quote is from one of my favorite books of his, *The Shattered Lantern: Rediscovering a Felt Presence of God* (New York: Crossroad, 2005).

37. Brueggemann, *Sabbath as Resistance,* 107.

Simplicity

1. Luke 12v15.

2. In the same teaching: Luke 12v33.

3. Matthew 6v25, 33.

4. Mark 4v19.

5. Matthew 19v24.

6. 1 Timothy 6v19.

7. He uses this phrase regularly, but his best-known work is *Simulacra and Simulation: The Body, in Theory: Histories of Cultural Materialism* (Ann Arbor, MI: University of Michigan Press, 1994).

8. Matthew 6v24. Okay, I'm taking liberty here. The NIV correctly translates it "money"; older translations have "mammon."

9. Quoted by Jeremy Lent in *The Patterning Instinct: A Cultural History of Humanity's Search for Meaning* (New York: Prometheus Books, 2017), 380. (Note: this is the beginning of the now-common business idea of planned obsolescence, also known as why you want a new iPhone *every* fall.)

10. Wayne Muller, *Sabbath: Finding Rest, Renewal, and Delight in Our Busy Lives* (New York: Bantam, 2000), 130. I got this and the Cowdrick quote from *The Century of the Self,* a telling 2002 BBC documentary by Adam Curtis you can watch for free on YouTube, https://youtube.com/watch?time_continue=9&v=eJ3RzGoQC4s.

11. Margot Alder, "Behind the Ever-Expanding American Dream House," NPR, July 4, 2006, www.npr.org/templates/story/story.php?storyId=5525283.

12. President George W. Bush on October 11, 2001, "Bush Shopping Quote," C-SPAN video clip, www.c-span.org/video/?c4552776/bush-shopping-quote.

13. These ads are from a simple Google search of "advertising in the 1800s."

14. For an overview of his story, read Edward Bernays, *Propaganda* (Morrisville, NC: Lulu, 2017), or watch the BBC documentary *The Century of Self.*

15. Bernays, *Propaganda,* 1.

16. Four thousand is the number that's thrown out, but it's hard to know because a great deal of it depends on how much TV you watch and how much time you spend on your phone. Here's a great summary of the research: Bryce Sanders, "Do We Really See 4,000 Ads a Day?," *The Business Journals,* September 1, 2017, www.bizjournals.com/bizjournals/how-to/marketing/2017/09/do-we-really-see-4-000-ads-a-day.html. Whatever the number is, it's really high.

17. Mark Twain, *More Maxims of Mark* (Privately printed, 1927).

18. Gregg Easterbrook, *The Progress Paradox: How Life Gets Better While People Feel Worse* (New York: Random House, 2003), 163.

19. 1 Timothy 6v8.

20. Jennifer Robison, "Happiness Is Love—and $75,000," Gallup, November 17, 2011, http://news.gallup.com/businessjournal/150671/happiness-is-love-and-75k.aspx.

21. Richard J. Foster, *Freedom of Simplicity: Finding Harmony in a Complex World* (New York: HarperOne, 2005), 215.

22. John de Graaf, David Wann, and Thomas Naylor, *Affluenza: How Overconsumption Is Killing Us—and How to Fight Back* (San Francisco: Berrett-Koehler, 2014). Best I can tell, the word *affluenza* was first used in 1954 and then gained traction in a PBS documentary from 1997 by the same name. You can locate more information about the PBS show at https://pbs.org/kcts/affluenza.

23. Psalm 39v6.

24. Alan Fadling, *An Unhurried Life: Following Jesus' Rhythms of Work and Rest* (Downers Grove, IL: InterVarsity Press, 2013), 48. I came across this book after I'd already finished the first draft of this book, and I started laughing. It's basically this book, only smarter and better. If this book strikes a chord with you, I encourage you to read Fadling's book next.

25. Again, Thomas R. Kelly in *A Testament of Devotion* (New York: HarperCollins, 1992), viii.

26. A fascinating read on the disappearance of moral and spiritual knowledge from our culture is *Knowing Christ Today: Why We Can Trust Spiritual Knowledge* (New York: Harper-One, 2009) by Dallas Willard. It's about how morality and spirituality have been moved from the realm of knowledge to the realm of opinion and feeling in our culture, and how hopelessly untrue that secular view of reality is.

27. Acts 20v35.

28. Matthew 6v24.

29. Luke 12v15.

30. Chuck Palahniuk, *Fight Club* (New York: Norton, 1996). Yes, I know this book is vulgar and uncouth. It is also written by a Portlander and one of the best books I've ever read, so somehow I justify it. And no, I've not seen the movie.

31. Matthew 6v19–21.

32. Matthew 6v22–23.

33. Matthew 6v24.

34. Richard Rohr, *Adam's Return: The Five Promises of Male Initiation* (New York: Crossroad, 2016).

35. Matthew 6v25.

36. Now, I'm not against organizing. I read Marie Kondo's *The Life-Changing Magic of Tidying Up: The Japanese Art of Decluttering and Organizing* (Berkeley: Ten Speed Press, 2014) along with millions of other Americans with too much crap in their closets, and I loved it. But while there are minimalism overtones in it, it's not really a book on minimalism. It's a book on organizing.

37. Joshua Becker, *Clutterfree with Kids: Change Your Thinking, Discover New Habits, Free Your Home* (2014), 31.

38. Foster, *Freedom of Simplicity,* 8.

39. Mark Scandrette, *Free: Spending Your Time and Money on What Matters Most* (Downers Grove, IL: InterVarsity Press, 2013), 37.

40. Henry David Thoreau, *Walden* (Edinburgh, UK: Black & White Classics, 2014), 51–52.

41. C. F. Kelley, *The Spiritual Maxims of St. Francis de Sales* (Harlow, UK: Longmans, Green, 1954).

42. The Minimalists, again.

Joshua Fields Millburn and Ryan Nicodemus, *Essential: Essays by the Minimalists* (Missoula, MT: Asymmetrical, 2015).

43. Marie Kondo, *Spark Joy: An Illustrated Master Class on the Art of Organizing and Tidying Up* (Berkeley: Ten Speed Press, 2016).

44. Joshua Becker, *The More of Less: Finding the Life You Want Under Everything You Own* (Colorado Springs, CO: Water-Brook, 2016), 87.

45. Annalyn Censky, "Americans Make Up Half of the World's Richest 1%," CNN Money, January 4, 2012, http://money .cnn.com/2012/01/04/news /economy/world_richest/index .htm.

46. 1 Timothy 6v17–19. I find this worth putting to memory. Or at least sticking somewhere you'll see it periodically.

47. Luke 8v1–3.

48. Matthew 11v19.

49. John 19v23.

50. Foster, *Freedom of Simplicity,* 58.

51. See, for example, Matthew 5–7, where all through the

Sermon on the Mount Jesus ends each teaching with a practice—leave your gift at the altar and go be reconciled (5v24), go an extra mile with the Roman soldier (v41), wash your face and put oil on your head when you're fasting (6v17), etc.

52. Robynne Boyd, "One Footprint at a Time," *Scientific American* (blog), July 14, 2011, https://blogs.scientificamerican.com/plugged-in/httpblogsscientificamericancomplugged-in20110714one-footprint-at-a-time.

53. For these stats and a mind-blowing documentary on the issue, watch *The True Cost,* Life Is My Movie Entertainment, 2015, https://truecostmovie.com. We hosted a screening of this film at our church. This is an area of social justice where there's still a lot of awareness raising that needs to be done.

54. William Morris, *William Morris on Art and Socialism* (North Chelmsford, MA: Courier Corporation, 1999), 53.

55. From Tertullian. And also, "You Romans hold nothing in common except your wives." Boom.

56. The best one I've come across that is explicitly Christian is in *Free* by Mark Scandrette. Phenomenal resource to put the ideas of this chapter into practice.

57. Ecclesiastes 2v24.

58. See what I did there? I've quoted Richard Foster so many times in this chapter I have to mix it up and call him Quaker, lest you realize I'm just quoting the same smart person over and *over* again. Richard J. Foster, *Celebration of Discipline: The Path to Spiritual Growth* (San Francisco: HarperCollins, 1998), 92.

59. Yet *another* quote from Richard Foster in *Freedom of Simplicity,* 72. Read it!

60. This great idea is from Dallas Willard, *The Great Omission: Reclaiming Jesus's Essential Teachings on Discipleship* (New York: HarperCollins, 2006), a good introduction to Willard's ideas, especially if you don't read a lot. It's his shortest book.

61. Philippians 4v13, ESV.

62. Philippians 4v11–12.

63. Arthur M. Schlesinger, *The Cycles of American History* (New York: Houghton Mifflin Harcourt, 1999), 27.

64. This is used throughout *Ecclesiastes,* starting in 1v14.

Slowing

1. To clarify, there is a sense in which spontaneity and flexibility is healthy and helpful on the spiritual journey, especially as we grow older. Cue a book someday on active and passive spirituality, the second half of life, aging, and Henri Nouwen's definition of maturity as "being led where you would rather not go." Henri Nouwen, *In the Name of Jesus: Reflections on Christian Leadership* (New York: Crossroad, 1989). Someday . . .

2. Jane McGonigal, *Super-Better: The Power of Living Gamefully* (New York: Penguin, 2016).

3. David Zach, as quoted by Richard A. Swenson, in *Margin: Restoring Emotional, Physical, Financial, and Time Reserves to Overloaded Lives* (Colorado Springs, CO: NavPress, 2004), 112.

4. Let's start a movement, shall we? No hashtag necessary. Just drop "I'm practicing the spiritual discipline of slowing" at your next watercooler chat.

5. John Ortberg, *The Life You've Always Wanted: Spiritual Disciplines for Ordinary People* (Grand Rapids, MI: Zondervan, 2002), 83.

6. When Jesus teaches on the spiritual disciplines in Matthew 6, he mentions three by name: prayer, fasting, and almsgiving— what most first-century rabbis taught were the three core spiritual disciplines.

7. Psalm 34v8.

8. It's dated now but still worth reading: Jake Knapp, "My Year with a Distraction-Free iPhone (and How to Start Your Own Experiment)," Time Dorks, August 30, 2014, https://medium.com/time-dorks/my-year-with-a-distraction-free-iphone-and-how-to-start-your-own-experiment-6ff74a0e7a50.

9. Meena Hart Duerson, "We're

Addicted to Our Phones: 84% Worldwide Say They Couldn't Go a Single Day Without Their Mobile Device in Their Hand," *New York Daily News,* August 16, 2012, www.nydailynews .com/life-style/addicted-phones -84-worldwide-couldn-single -day-mobile-device-hand-article -1.1137811; and Mary Gorges, "90 Percent of Young People Wake Up with Their Smart-phones," Ragan, December 21, 2012, www.ragan.com/90 -percent-of-young-people-wake -up-with-their-smartphones.

10. John Koblin, "How Much Do We Love TV? Let Us Count the Ways," *New York Times,* June 30, 2016, www.nytimes.com /2016/07/01/business/media /nielsen-survey-media-viewing .html.

11. Koblin, "How Much Do We Love TV?"

12. Rina Raphael, "Netflix CEO Reed Hastings: Sleep Is Our Competition: For Netflix, the Battle for Domination Goes Far Beyond Which TV Remote to Pick Up," Fast Company, November 6, 2017, www

.fastcompany.com/40491939 /netflix-ceo-reed-hastings-sleep -is-our-competition.

13. Byung-Chul Han, *The Burnout Society* (Stanford: Stanford University Press, 2015), 12–13.

14. Walter Brueggemann, *Sabbath as Resistance: Saying No to the Culture of Now* (Louisville, KY: Westminster John Knox Press, 2014), 67.

15. That would be Socrates.

16. John Mark Comer, "Silence & Solitude: Part 1, The Basics," Practicing the Way, https: //practicingtheway.org/silence -solitude/week-one.

17. Timothy Keller, *Prayer: Experiencing Awe and Intimacy with God* (New York: Dutton, 2014), 147.

18. Marilyn Gardner, "The Ascent of Hours on the Job," *Christian Science Monitor,* May 2, 2005, www.csmonitor.com /2005/0502/p14s01-wmgn.html.

19. Sima Shakeri, "8 Days Is the Perfect Vacation Length, Study Says," *HuffPost,* September 17, 2017, www.huffingtonpost .ca/2017/09/15/8-days-is-the

-perfect-vacation-length-study
-says_a_23211082.

Epilogue: A quiet life

1. AA made this famous, but it's from the "Serenity Prayer" by Reinhold Niebuhr. "5 Timeless Truths from the Serenity Prayer That Offer Wisdom in the Modern Age," *HuffPost,* December 6, 2017, https://huffingtonpost.com/2014/03/18/serenity-prayer-wisdom_n_4965139.html.

2. Brother Lawrence, *The Practice of the Presence of God* (Eastford, CT: Martino Fine Books, 2016).

3. From one of my all-time favorite reads: Frank Laubach, *Letters by a Modern Mystic* (Colorado Springs: Purposeful Design Publications, 2007), 15. It's not really a book, just a little forty-five-page collection of journal entries and letters. Worth your time.

4. C. S. Lewis, *The Complete C. S. Lewis Signature Classics* (San Francisco: HarperOne, 2002), 155.

5. William Stafford, "You Reading This, Be Ready," *Ask Me: 100 Essential Poems* (Minneapolis, MN: Graywolf Press, 2014).

6. "5 Timeless Truths."

7. See the beatitudes of Matthew 5v3–12: "Blessed *are* . . . ," not "Blessed *will be when* . . . "

8. Psalm 23v6.

9. Edward H. Friedman, *A Failure of Nerve: Leadership in the Age of the Quick Fix* (New York: Church Publishing, 2017), 247. This is mentioned several times throughout Friedman's book.

10. 1 Thessalonians 4v11.

11. Jesuit Spiritual Center at Milford, https://jesuitspiritual-center.com/ignatian-spirituality.

12. 2 Timothy 4v6–7.

13. John Ortberg, *Soul Keeping: Caring for the Most Important Part of You* (Grand Rapids, MI: Zondervan, 2014), 126.

14. 2 Timothy 3v13.

Thanks for reading *The Ruthless Elimination of Hurry.*

A few things about me…

I live and work in Portland, Oregon, with my wife, T, and our three kids.

I'm the pastor for teaching and vision at Bridgetown Church. Our church is built around the very simple idea of practicing the way of Jesus, together, in Portland.

As for education, I hold a master's degree in biblical and theological studies from Western Seminary, and I'm currently at work on a doctorate in spiritual formation through Fuller Seminary and the Dallas Willard Center.

You're welcome to follow my teachings via the Bridgetown Church podcast or *This Cultural Moment,* a podcast I cohost with my friend Mark Sayers on following Jesus in the post-Christian world.

Find more at johnmarkcomer.com.